G a m e   a t   5 o

Game at 50 (and Beyond): Secret Seduction Tips for the Older Man

W. Nanner Flint

ii

Game at 50 (and Beyond): Secret Seduction Tips for the Older Man

Publisher's Cataloging-In-Publication Data
(Prepared by The Donohue Group, Inc.)

   Flint, W. Nanner.
   Game at 50 (and beyond) : secret seduction tips for the older man / W. Nanner Flint.

   p. ; cm.

   Includes bibliographical references.
   ISBN: 978-0-9910476-0-4

   1. Dating (Social customs) 2. Middle-aged men. 3. Man-woman relationships. 4. Courtship. I. Title. II. Title: Game at fifty (and beyond)

HQ801 .F55 2013
646.7/7/0844

Contents

Chapter 1

It Can Happen to You

It can happen to you. Or it has happened to you.

I was 50 years old. Happily married. Had just moved to the Midwest with a great paying job. My wife was going to tie up loose ends and travel in just a few months. Our financial struggles would soon be over. But her arrival date kept getting put back. She decided that moving wasn't a good idea. We should have a place to come back to, if not a house, an apartment. It would always be our home. So I put down cash to buy a place but then we needed more cash for the furniture and the arrival date was delayed again and then there was refurbishing the place and getting everything set up. She had to stay and supervise everything, of course. The minute it was all paid for I got the call.

"Don't you see that there is something wrong with our marriage?"

A year later I am sitting in a bar by myself working on my second drink and trying to figure out what went wrong.

Yes, it can happen to you. Dating in your 50's—or later—isn't that easy. Hell, it's tough. Very tough.

You lose half your friends in the divorce and then half of the half you kept because they're married and married people don't socialize with single people. You just haven't realized this yet. At first it seems strange to be the odd man out but then you realize that you are always the odd man out.

There are fewer and fewer invitations—you're responsible to some extent for this happening because after your divorce you're hardly your best self–and you come to think of that bar stool as your own. There are lots of people having fun in the bar but you aren't one of them.

You may meet a few women but starting to date again after being out of the market for so long is not easy. It's painful. You don't know how to dress; you don't know where to go. You do what you have always done, hitting the happy hours at places you used to go while you were married. It's a miracle you don't run into your ex, but most of the people at those places are already coupled up. And what about Saturdays?

On Saturdays everyone is coupled up. It's like all of a sudden the week only has one night. And if you can't get anything going on that night, nothing is going to happen. So Saturday night's date is with the television and there's nothing to watch.

And then you remember that friend of your ex's who always complained about how she couldn't get a date and that there weren't enough nice guys and why can't I meet a guy like you? But when you called her after the divorce and three martinis she didn't even pick up.

Or you've done all the things you did when you were in your 20's; you go to nightclubs and the girls are delicious but they are so young and when you approach them it's "ewww" and then you realize it's three in the morning and you've put in almost a full shift drinking. This cannot possibly be the way to find a relationship.

And it isn't.

It doesn't have to be this way. I've already gone though it. I can give you the benefit of my experience so you can avoid the mistakes I've made. You can take a little time and learn what to do or you can waste time going to bars and wondering why nothing is working. Or you can buy a book like *The Game* and after reading it wonder why there is so little for the older guy.

I went through all these things and I learned what to do. I am now sharing this information with you. I don't consider myself a player, but I know how to get phone numbers. Others have told me that they cannot believe my successes. There was the opera singer, the school teacher, the lawyer; the CEO, the young mother with a baby at home and finally, the 19 year-old lesbian. And this doesn't count the various others that I chose not to let progress any farther.

You don't have to sit and drown your sorrows. You can get out there. This book shows you how.

CHAPTER 2

After the Divorce

They say that with divorce you lose a family but gain a nightclub. There is a good deal of truth in this, but still.

So you're divorced. Big deal. There are lots of women out there, you've heard the stories. When you were married you envied your single friends who went out all the time. Now you have the freedom to explore, to do whatever you want, to be free of having to explain yourself or cover your tracks or make up stories to paper over awkward situations that could be misunderstood.

Now you are alone. No one cares where you go, what you do or who you do it with. At first that freedom leads to going out every single night. More often than not, you end up coming home alone. You have been out of the dating scene for so long that you don't know what to do.

Before there was always a structure for meeting new people–school, work–but now that is gone. You can't date at work with the sexual harassment laws the way they are now–so forget about capitalizing on Cosmopolitan magazine's advice to young women to find sexual partners at the workplace.

But you look around and it seems that there are few alternatives in this world of new rules. What to do?

CHAPTER 3

The Pathetic Pub Crawl

I didn't know how to meet women. I was shy. I didn't know what to say. Picking up women is a skill others had, but not me. I had no idea what to do. I figured that if you simply hung out you would meet people as if by magic. My favorite place was Tu Tu Tango in Coconut Grove–it's now closed–and I sat in the bar, secretly hoping that she would show up and we would talk and everything would be as it was before.

Pathetic.

So I started riding a circuit, or bar hopping. I'd start the evening at Books and Books. This was a relatively sedate place, a bookstore with a bar.   I would have a glass of wine and then try to figure out where to go next. The Coral Gables entertainment district–it's not called that of course–consists of a dozen places within a few blocks radius, so it seemed a perfect place to find variety. If one place was dead there was another. The crowd was older so this seemed to make more sense.

After Books and Books I'd head off to Doc Dammer's and have a drink there.   There were a few occasions when I'd strike up a conversation–the liquor helped, actually–but usually it was just me and the barstool. Then off to Houston's, on the corner of the Miracle Mile. It was always hopping. There wasn't any music but nevertheless it was loud. There was no place to sit at the bar and so you had to stand.   But mostly I was standing by myself. You just can't approach a group, right? So eventually I would tire of the noise and lack of interaction.

The next destination was the Globe, a few blocks away, a strange travel agency and bar that had just gotten their full liquor license. In the evenings they had a jazz band or a pianist. But nothing happened there in the same way that nothing happened anywhere else I had visited. I'd walk around and go into another place if there were people and a pleasant vibe but after ten minutes I'd wonder what the hell I was doing there.

If I was downtown there was Novecento's on Brickell which was never empty. But usually I would go home first, change. I don't know why I bothered changing for all I ever did was take the tie off and lose the jacket. I usually started at Books and Books with a champagne pop, then walk over to Houston's to see if I could get in. Usually it was too crowded to make the effort. I would go across the street to Morton's but the crowd didn't come until later in the evening. Doc Dammer's, City Cellar or Tarpon Bend were sometimes worth a drink. The Globe was located a little bit farther away but you could usually find a halfway decent scene there. If I could get a seat at the bar it was worthwhile staying, if for no other reason to talk to the tattooed girl who tended bar.

If I was really desperate I would head to Smith and Wollensky's on the Beach. I had been told there was a singles scene there, but if there was, it was comprised of few women and lots of older single men just like me. Books and Books had music later so I would end my evening there.

I went to nightclubs but my timing was always off—go to a nightclub at 9 pm and you're the only one there. Go at 10 and the three of you can look at each other.

After all this frustration, what was there to do? Some head to Hooters or strip clubs as a solution. Going to these places is like going to a casino where there is never a payout.

Hooters is a place for hungry divorced dads. The chicken wings are great and the girls are pretty, but what's the point? If you are going to date a Hooter's gal it's because you met her outside and she just happens to work there. The pleasant smiles and tight uniforms are tools to earn tips. There's nothing wrong with the place, but if you think you are going to find a new girlfriend there, you are mistaken.

Strip clubs will just remind you of what you are missing. Avoid them. Even if you have enough money to have fun there, avoid them. If you have to, you can go after work with your buddies but that's it. As a single guy, going by yourself is a pathetic waste of time.

The only night when single guys are the majority of the customers in strip clubs is Saturday night. Maybe on Sundays as well. On Friday nights they are full of married guys worrying about the excuses they will make up for their wives. As a courtesy the dancers don't wear perfume. Once you've dropped a C-note–or more–you realize that you are standing at a slot machine with no payout. If you're going to insist on going despite my advice, at least make sure the place has decent food. Like chicken wings.

And by the way, I am totally against the concept of "decide what you want in a woman and pursue her." For a while I thought that what I needed was a woman with a medical degree. It's not like you can look through a catalog or select from a menu. You don't know who is out there. So why limit yourself? Just as whoever is out there doesn't know much about you.

CHAPTER 4

Old Man

I looked into the mirror and saw an old man. He was unfamiliar; he looked sort of like me but was a wholly different person. His hair was white–I could lie and say it was gray but the only time it looked gray was in the morning after getting out of the shower. I've been told that I don't have wrinkles, but what then were those things under my eyes? The flabbiness around my middle was testament to the cocktails that have more calories than vanilla milkshakes.

Who was this person? Who was this stranger? And whoever he is, is he the kind of person that a woman would want to meet?

I looked in the mirror at my own despair. This would never work.

In the beginning I did things on automatic pilot. On Friday nights when I was married I would always go to a happy hour with my wife. Now I kept doing so, but alone. It was a solitary pub crawl and I later realized that all I was doing was trying to replace what I had lost and I was failing miserably.

Usually if I saw a pretty or interesting woman I would simply hide behind my drink and say nothing. If there was an obvious conversational set-up or if she started talking to me, I would respond, but otherwise the only conversations I had were with bartenders.

I was drinking too much. Way too much. If you're going to hang out in bars for seven hours you are going to drink. I was going out after working, starting at five or at the latest by six. I came home at midnight or sometimes later. It was putting in a full shift of drinking. After a solid six or seven hours of drinking you are wasted. And the next day is shot.

I was pathetic.

The worst evening ended in a morning when I woke up with my shoes on in bed, fully-clothed. The house looked like it had been hit by a burglar. Bookshelves were overturned and somehow the computer monitor was screen-down on the floor. I looked outside and my car was gone. After a while I realized that meant that I hadn't driven home. I had called a friend from a bar and he realized that I was in no condition to drive home. He had picked me up and taken me home. I learned this later, because I didn't remember any of it. All I was doing was chasing an ex's ghost into a bottle. I was looking for what could not be found.

I was pathetic.

CHAPTER 5

Cobwebs on my Barstool

I kept having bad luck. Nothing was working and I felt that I cobwebs were starting to grow on the barstool. I couldn't possibly have been the only person in these circumstances. The last time I had done any serious dating was in college but this was different. You don't date in college anyway. The whole system is designed to organize what now is called "hooking up" but then was called meeting the opposite sex. People didn't date, there were mixers and then "deep meaningful relationships." Some couples that found each other then are still together today, years later.

People conveniently found each other in classes and through friends of friends, in college bars, at fraternity and sorority parties, a mixers, at wine and cheese parties, at football games, retreats and all of the myriad activities that universities sponsor during the four year party to bring people together.

You think that it will last forever but it does not. When your relationship fails you think you can just go back but there isn't any going back. When the music stops and you're left standing you have to go out and make your own opportunities. You still have a chance.

When 50 hits you're supposed to have an organized life. A spouse, family. This is what society expects of you. And it's something you want, though you're not sure why.

Why? Married people have more sex than single people. People in a relationship have more sex than people who are single. Single people have more variety and the grass always looks greener but there are dry spells. Lots of them. And each one seems longer than the last.

When the music stops, getting back into the

game isn't all that easy. The skills that you had once upon a time–they weren't skills at all. Basically you just had to show up. You were fishing at a pond full of fish that all wanted to be caught.

Now you find that you need real skills. That's what's missing. You try to think up a pickup line, a method to chat up women, a cool thing to say that will help you burrow your way into her heart and her bed.

There was no way that I was going to announce myself with some lame pick-up line. There's too much at stake. If the line falls flat–if one of her girlfriends makes a face–you strike out and if you're smart you make a hasty exit out the door.

I knew that there had to be a better way. Someone had to have studied this stuff. So I decided that I would do some research.

Today everybody knows about *The Game.* Before the book was published these subjects were not openly discussed. You may have a friend who always has been good with women but you had no idea what makes up the secret sauce, or even if there is a secret sauce. Maybe some guys are gifted or some are simply luckier than others.

After one of these long nights that I realized that I did not know what I was doing. I had no idea what I was doing. I didn't have a social life and "fun" is not a stumble-drunk returning home with no memory of what had happened before.

But like in the movie *Pulp Fiction*, every now and then you have a moment of pure clarity. I realized that I was not the only person in this situation. Others had dealt with it. Others had written about it.

I could learn from them.

So I went to the library.

CHAPTER 6

Academic Research

I started doing research almost immediately.

There is a good deal of works on this subject. The literature starts with Ovid's *Ars Amatoria* (The Art of Love) which was written over two thousand years ago but contains the insights of a contemporary. Ovid's advice and observations are valid today.

There are other books that have been written about the subject over the years. *The Arabian Nights* dates from the Ninth century, but wasn't the only Arabian love manual. Ibn Hazm's *The Ring of the Dove* was also written during the Muslim occupation of Spain.

The next appearance in the literature is Baltasar Gracian, whose *The Art of Worldly Wisdom* addressed the subject in 1637 in Renaissance Spain. Spain also is the source of the seducer Don Juan, a character whose name is now a synonym for "womanizer". Tirso de Molina's play, *The Trickster of Seville* was first performed in 1630. Roughly around this time in China the *Chin P'ing Mei* (*The Golden Lotus*) addressed these subjects from a wholly different cultural perspective.

Les Liaisons Dangereuses provided a French model in 1782 but while this text contains much wisdom concerning male-female relationships it is hardly a practical guide. Cyrano de Bergerac is a story about a dating coach. One would think that the 1800 or so pages of the memoirs of the great seducer, Giacomo Casanova, would be full of helpful tips. There are a few, such as the " man who makes known his love by words is a fool." Casanova also suggests how to convince two girls to engage in a threesome. You will find that tidbit at the end of this book.

After Casanova there seems to be a gap—where little or nothing was written about the subject. Books failed to find a publisher, were suppressed, or did not survive. Dating manuals fall into the category of bibliographic ephemera. In any event, the point of my research was not to write an academic thesis, it was to find practical advice that I could use.

Scientology grew out of a self-help book which most forget made the New York Times bestseller list for a while in the 1950's. It is fairly well known that the founder of Scientology, L. Ron Hubbard, was a follower of Aleister Crowley and participated in what in the 70's would have been called swinging parties but in the late 40's in Los Angeles was called a "sex cult." I could not find a Scientology text which addresses the subject of dating. Though the group today is concerned with using the mind to alter your own reality favorably, if Ron learned how to pick up girls he kept the secrets to himself.

The sexual revolution of the 1960's started with contraceptive pill and continued on to the Summer of Love in San Francisco. As Philip Larkin put it,

> Sexual intercourse began
> In nineteen sixty-three
> (which was rather late for me) -
> Between the end of the "Chatterley"
>   ban
> And the Beatles' first LP.
>
> Up to then there'd only been
> A sort of bargaining,
> A wrangle for the ring,
> A shame that started at sixteen
> And spread to everything.

from *Annus Mirabilis*

A popular anti-draft poster from the 1960's read, "Girls Say 'Yes' to Boys who Say 'No.'" Was dating really so easy then? If all you had to do was pretend to be avoiding the draft to get laid, you did not need much game at all. During the days of free love, sex was, well, free.

The 60's were followed by a time of retreat and introspection. Free love came to an end, marijuana became harder drugs and we woke up to the hangover of the 70's. The EST movement was about personal empowerment but meeting new people played a significant role. New books dealt with those challenges. In 1970 Eric Weber wrote a book entitled, *How to Pick-up Girls*.

Neuro-linguistic programming introduced concepts such as "mirroring" and matching the breathing patterns of someone you want to persuade. It wasn't long before these techniques were discovered by what has come to be known as the "seduction community." Now the literature was starting to reach critical mass. Ross Jeffries wrote, *Secrets of Speed Seduction*.

The term "sarging" was coined by Jeffries' disciples and named after his cat, Sarge. "Sarging" describes going out on the town with the specific intention of meeting new women. It is not about hanging out with your friends–though your friends might well tag along–to drown your sorrows over beers or discuss the sorry state of the Dolphins. This, instead, is purposeful activity. There is otherwise no hidden meaning to the term.

A Jeffries disciple, David D'Angelo, wrote a book called, *Double your Dating*. Blogging was in the process of being born in the 1990's, but what has now come to be known as the "seduction community" started coalescing around Usenet, building a vocabulary and sharing tips.

Finally Neil Strauss dove into these resources and wrote *The Game* and the world of the PUA (pick-up artist) entered the collective consciousness. Before Strauss there was Robert Greene's *The Art of Seduction*. If *The Game* is a field manual, Greene's *Seduction* is the college textbook.

But in all my research I never came across any book written specifically for the older man. This book will hopefully fill that gap.

When I started this research, Strauss had not written *The Game*. That was still in the future. But otherwise the information was out there. It was merely a question of acquiring and field-testing the new information.

I am not going to tell you to sit in the library reading Roman poetry if you plan on getting laid tonight. If you're going out sarging you are better off flipping through an issue of People magazine or the National Enquirer instead. It will be much more useful. But if you can, spend some time with the literature. You may come away from each text or guidebook with only one useful point, such as Casanova's threesome strategy, but over time your skill set will grow.

As you read through the literature, you will start to get a feel for the craft. With experience you will start to see which techniques are impossible or silly as well as which ones are intriguing and might work for you.

Sometimes the advice seems daunting. Reading *The Game* will make you think that game is all about memorizing routines and scripts, to the point where students of the book stuff cheat sheets in their pockets to refer to before they go out sarging. Let me say this–if you have to pull a notecard out of your pocket at a bar before you can talk to a woman you are in deep trouble. You can expect her to ask what's on the paper. You could hide the cheat sheet on your phone or wear an earpiece like you are a Secret Service agent while having a friend feed you lines, but why? These crutches provide false courage.

You don't have to memorize a script. You cannot be looking down at a phone all the time when you are trying to have a conversation with someone. If you think you have to memorize a script, go ahead, but keep in mind that you will not be able to predict half of the conversation. Instead, there will be three parts to your performance: what you plan to say, what you actually say and what you wished you had said.

What does an actor do when another actor

stops following the script? Unless they've both agreed to ad lib, usually he stands there like a deer in the headlights not knowing what to do. Within sixty seconds your planned script will go out the window no matter how well you think you know it. The last thing you want to do or be is caught in the headlights.

The takeaway from all of my study was that these issues have been addressed and the problems for the most part have been solved. Others had been in the same position in which I found myself. They knew what to do and I could learn from them. After a while, I could internalize the knowledge so that it became second nature and I could add my own personal twists. Some of these I found extraordinarily powerful. You will too.

CHAPTER 7

The Art of War

Not all women approach dating in a calculated fashion. They may have their list of things they want in a man, lists that they have been drawing up since they were 14. What people say they want is very different from what they actually pursue. You wonder why a woman says, "I want a nice guy who will treat me like a lady and take me to nice places" before falling for the weirdo in the leather jacket who makes faces whenever she talks. The only place he took her to was the men's room in the disco on a promise of a line of cocaine. Why is it that a nice guy with a good job can't get a date? Why is that a U.S. citizen in a sea of illegal immigrants can't find a woman who needs marriage in order to stay in the country? If all the women want walks on the beach why aren't the beaches as crowded as 5th Avenue in NYC at lunchtime?

Women don't want nice guys. Perhaps in some intellectual sense they do, but read enough romance novels and you find that what they are attracted to is the pirate, the alpha male. You're in middle management and you've been there for a long time. It's been a long time since you were a buccaneer, if you ever were. Now is the time to be a pirate. Forget about being nice. The astonishing thing is that while women will complain about how men are shits and why aren't there any nice guys, they keep coming back for more. They can't get the pirate out of their minds.

Men are exactly the opposite. We don't say we want a nice girl. We want a tramp. A woman who is independent with her own successful career scares us. A woman who can cook and who can run a home like a business that turns a profit each year is uninteresting. Yeah, sure, she's wonderful but our eyes are wandering to the trampy looking miniskirted babe flirtatiously lighting a cigaret with the short leather jacket and gravity-defying heels. Her experience in cooking is limited to reheating leftovers in the microwave. While she too says that she is interested in finding a nice guy, we know better.

But you're not that pirate and the miniskirted girl leaning over the pool table is definitely not paying any attention to you. What to do?

CHAPTER 8

Don't Change Yourself

Body

You need to take a physical self-inventory. Many will tell you that a makeover is needed. Many dating books will tell you to hit the gym, buy new clothes and get a haircut. That advice may be excellent for twenty-something chumps who can't seem to put down the game controller to get their lives organized, but for us over-50's it tends to be more metaphorical than anything else. After a lifetime of lethargy, you are not going to see any significant results after six weeks in the gym. There's not a great point in getting a new haircut if you don't have the hair in the first place. You don't need a set of disco duds if you're not going to nightclubs. And so forth.

The essential takeaway of the need for a self-inventory is a good idea. Physical exercise is never a bad thing and sex is physically demanding–if it's not, you're doing it wrong. A visit to the cardiologist is not a bad way to make sure that you have the strength for all your upcoming exertions.

Forget cosmetic changes. I know. You hate health clubs and gyms. They're loud, it's all about looks, you don't look that great. Don't worry. You are not going to the gym to change your looks. You are going for a different reason. This is your motivator: you need to go to prepare for the physical demands of fucking.

Ramp up with a modest program of exercise. Perhaps fifteen minutes a day, working yourself up to thirty after a while. You will not see any dramatic changes. You may not see any changes at all. You may simply slow age-related weight gain and that in itself is not a bad idea. But you will get stronger and strength is what you need. Go to a co-ed gym. A gym is not a great place to meet people, but it's not a bad one either. You might meet someone there and at least you will have working out in common.

If you let your spouse buy clothes for you while you were married–and who doesn't-now is the time to make wardrobe changes. Throw out half of what is in your closet. Keep your business clothes and a few casual shirts and jeans. Throw out the rest. Good Will, the Salvation Army, Faith Farm and others will be happy to take your old clothes off your hands. If you're like me, the closet was full of clothes that she liked and that I kind of liked but not really.

Buy clothes for you. Start now. Because the wife-bought clothes for the most part are still on hangars, much of it is out of style anyway. You don't have to fill the closet all at once, you can do so gradually. If you don't know what to buy, you can get tips from the women you meet. Clothes are an easy conversational topic.

Going to the mall on a shopping trip is a non-threatening meet-up for a woman who gave you her number last weekend.

Shoes are more important than you think. Men do not pay all that much attention to shoes beyond making sure that track shoes aren't worn with suits (at least, not all the time.). Shoes for women are a much more serious matter. Chinese culture institutionalized the foot fetish for over two thousand years. There must be something to it. Shoes are like catnip for women. They like going shopping for shoes, looking at pictures of shoes, pinning pictures of shoes on Pinterest, talking about shoes to their friends and thinking about shoes they would like to buy or wear that evening.

I honestly have no idea why women focus on shoes so much, but they do. The reason why it is important for you is that they check out men's shoes as well. They assume that since shoes are important for women they must be important for men. It is usually a huge surprise when they find out that is not the case.

Once a college student complained to me about how he was having no luck in finding a girlfriend, that all he did was hang out with his buddies, that what do women want, what's wrong with me?–the usual litany. You can't tell a college kid to stop dressing like a slob–his friends will think he's gone off the deep end. Upgrading the college male dress code will have to wait for after graduation day. On the other hand, and this is what I told him–"when you go out, put on a nice pair of shoes, preferably clean. Girls will pay attention." A small detail, perhaps, but it worked for him.

So when you go out, by all means leave your tennis shoes in the closet. Unless, of course, you are going to a place or a party where that kind of footwear is common. And if you do, make sure that you have a new pair and that they are clean.

The reason why you need to start going to the gym is not so that you'll have six pack abs but so that your cardiovascular system can handle physical exertion (i.e., sex) for more than two minutes. If you can't walk for five minutes on a treadmill, how do you expect to thrust for that amount of time? Strength is strength, and if you can get winded on the treadmill you will be winded in the sack.

So it's not necessarily about improving your looks (though if you can take off a bit of flab, good for you) it's about becoming more physical, or being able to endure intense physical exertion. This is the real reason why you need to go to the gym. It has nothing to do with improving your looks or improving your confidence. You simply need to be strong. You won't get that by sitting on the couch.

But be careful not to go too far.

The advice in this book is not a one-size fits all formula. Think of it as a menu from which you can pick and choose. One man who styled himself a player always sprayed a little women's perfume on himself before he went out. His theory was twofold: first, women like the smell, so he figured this would make them feel comfortable around him. Secondly, women know that men do not wear women's perfume and this means that a woman had been around him. The point wasn't that his new acquaintance would become jealous of the phantom other woman, but figure that if she had been around him, that he was safe, more or less. So the perfume provided a form of validation. I'm not suggesting that guys load up on Chanel No. 5 before going out. But if it works for you, who am I to say no?

Mind

Popular culture is important. You need to have a grasp of it to converse comfortably with strangers. Current events are tricky since politics might make the discussion serious. When you are out having a good time you really do not want to discuss the consequences of going off the gold standard and the dangers of inflation or deflation, the Great Recession of 2008, trade imbalances or the latest regional conflict.

Keep it light.

Fortunately, popular culture always provides fodder for light conversations, whether it's the Kardashians, television series, cartoons or a scandal. These are subjects on which everyone has an opinion but no one truly cares. People usually have no problem expressing an opinion on these issues and such conversations are infinitely better than conversations about the weather. People talk about the weather when they want to have a conversation but have nothing to say. These topics will get the conversation going or keep it going.

It's not a bad idea to look at sources such as People Magazine, Vogue, TMZ or E! to stay abreast of this kind of news. It used to be that you had to drop a $20 bill to buy an armful of magazines in order to stay current, but now it's simply a question of visiting a few web sites since the kind of news you want is is the kind which always percolates to the top.

In the movie *Planes, Trains and Automobiles* there's a scene where John Candy is trying to get a busload of people to sing and no one knows the same songs. Then he starts in with "Meet the Flintstones" and everyone joins in. Popular culture is like that, we all share it so there is no reason not to use it.

Some crafty men read women's magazines for the purpose of keeping up with what's important to women today. Generally I don't believe that reading women's magazines is going to be of much use. There is always a current fashion that people will have an opinion about but it's probably not necessary to read a magazine to find out about it.

Women's magazines can be very useful when it comes to learning women's perspectives on relationships and how to keep them alive and meeting men and the rest. It may give you ideas about what women think are good places to meet men that you haven't considered.

Once such an article almost got me sent to the ends of the earth. There was an article in the *Miami Herald*-back in the day when people still got their news from newspapers-about dating after 50 and a wine bar in my neighborhood was mentioned. I had never considered it, for some reason. I met an Argentine girl there who after our second date wanted me to go with her to a town called Ushuaia, one of the closest cities to Antarctica in the Americas. We had just met. It all seemed a little extreme. My conclusion was that anything can happen in a wine bar.

The Game is popular culture too. Memories are short, but for a while after Neil Strauss' book came out you couldn't run a "best friends test" without getting supercilious looks, a rolling of the eyes and a comment about kino or "aren't you supposed to neg me?" This is a reason that too formulaic Game is ineffective. Women read these books too.

Looking at women's magazines will teach you that women run game on us. What is an article titled, "How to Get a Guy to Commit" if not game? Once your eyes are open you will see dozens of articles about female game. Is makeup game? Shoes? Fashion? Sun Tzu in his *Art of War* said, "Know your enemy." This was good advice two thousand years ago and it is good advice today. Women simply have another word for game. That word is "flirting".

Miami was somewhat insulated for a while because of the time it took to translate the book into Spanish. If you're running game it really doesn't matter whether your new friend is familiar with the book or not. Like it or not, these are mating rituals and to a great extent are hard wired in us.

Seduction suggests overcoming someone's will and that is not what game is about. If a woman lets herself be seduced, who is really doing the seducing? A man may well think that he has seduced a woman because initially she rebuffed his attentions. A woman can say "not now" in so many ways. But if attraction is there she will be intrigued and sometimes, but not always, she may start to pay attention. If a rapport is established which leads to companionship or even sex, there has been no seduction.

No one's will has been overcome.

I once read a post in /r/seduction by a woman who had studied game. She knew the routines back and forth and tried to put down a guy who tried to run game on her. But it didn't work. She commented, "I don't really know what happened, but next I know I was laughing and having a good time even though I could tell what he was doing." The insight here is that it really doesn't matter. Even if she knows what you are doing, you can still do it. She can, of course, walk away, but if she doesn't, well, it's game on.

On another occasion, I told a very skeptical female friend that I was putting my thoughts together to write this book. I told her, modestly, that I have made some contributions to the literature and she asked me, "like what?" So I told her about some of the secrets in this book. "Oh, that will never work," she said, "I can see right through that." So I told her that is because she is such a player herself. Next thing you know we're both laughing and having a good time. I could have asked her for her number if I didn't have it already.

CHAPTER 9

No Longer Twenty

You are no longer 20. The main point here is don't pretend that you still are. It won't work. When you go out, don't dress young, but don't dress old, either. Don't expect that you can go out all night to nightclubs. You won't be able to. If you do, you may find yourself falling asleep. If this happens, it's embarrassing. You need to step out of your comfort zone from time to time, but you can't be in the club at 4 am if you've got to be at work in a few hours.

You're better off restricting this type of experimentation to vacations. At least when you're on vacation you don't have to worry about sleeping in the next morning. Vacations are times when people let go more than in their workaday lives. You can do so as well.

If you have cash, don't be afraid to spend it. If you find yourself in a long line trying to get into a club, go to the front of the line and discreetly offer the doorman a gratuity. "Is there someway you could work things out so I don't have to wait in line? I'd be very grateful" is usually all you need to say. The amount of the gratuity depends on where you live. The thirty-something with you will wonder how you did it, the forty-something will think you are a cool guy for passing the line and the fifty-something will be happy you're both inside. It's a win-win for everyone. Don't be surprised, though, when you get in, to find a club that is nearly empty. The velvet ropes and a long line is a marketing device used by club owners to show that the venue is a desirable place to visit.

If you really want to be the life of the party, order bottle service and start handing out free drinks or letting people fill their glasses for free. Soon there will be a small crowd around you–at least until the booze bottles are empty. You may make a few new friends this way, but be careful-it can be quite expensive. Regular stories are reported in the Miami press about out-of-towners who had come to Miami Beach, bypassed a line by ordering bottle service and found themselves with a $1000- or more-bill, a credit card decline and new accommodations courtesy of law enforcement .

Keep in mind that the liver metabolizes alcohol more slowly when you're older. Two or three drinks at 50 is like five or six when you were in your 20's.

Whenever you think how disgustingly expensive this is, picture yourself at a divorce mediation. The arbitrator is charging $400 per hour, your attorney, $300, her attorney $300. They expect you to pay up and no, none of them take credit cards. They haven't heard of credit cards. It will be cash only, thank you very much. And you don't get much for your thousand.

I know I can get at least three hours out of $1000 bottle service, so I'm ahead of the game. And I'm having more fun.

CHAPTER 10

Dog Years

After 50 your years are like dog years. Use them wisely. They are running out. There is no reason to wait. You can continue to stay at home and I guarantee that nothing will happen. Sex is not something you save up for old age.

I tend to be a tire-kicker. I am not thinking long-term relationship after the first date and if I am buying a car I go back to dealership more than once to seal the deal. In the flea market I will walk past a seller's stall a few times before picking up an item and making an offer.

At least, that's how I used to do things. But

not any more. After 50, keep in mind that if you go back, not only may the opportunity be lost but you have lost valuable time. As you get older, time is a vanishing commodity. Ever day you will have less. You have to capitalize on what you have and each day you have less than the day before.

There is no reason to obsess about this fact, but there is also no reason to engage in behaviors as you did when you were twenty and had all the time in the world. If you see something you like at the flea market, buy it. Agonizing about the decision for a month is one month less that you could have been on the road. If this attitude seems inappropriate or too impulsive all I can say is that a week from now it will be less so, and a year from now maybe you will get the point.If you like the car, get it.

What I am talking about here is how you operate on a day to day basis, how you lead your daily life. I am not suggesting that you should live in the moment because you might die tomorrow. All that leads to is reckless behavior, and behavior does have consequences. Just remember that the coins of time that you have in your pocket are being spent, day by day. Spend them wisely.

CHAPTER 11

No Knocks at the Door

Without interaction there can be no action. I can guarantee that staying at home in front of the television will only lead to more staying at home in front of the television. The chances of an eligible woman knocking on your door is exceedingly unlikely. Yet it can happen. Where are you living? If you have stay out in the suburbs you can only expect to see married people at dinner parties who invite their sad-sack single girlfriends who whine about how their last relationship ended badly. So you have to move.

When you stopped living together with your wife all you wanted to do was to get out, to get away. The plan wasn't focused on the where-to, it was focused on the where-from. The result of this is that even a hammock in a tree sounded attractive. One day you will wake up in that tree and ask, :"where the fuck am I?" You won't have a good answer. So where to move? There is only one place to go: the city. The courtesan embodies the heart of the city, or so it was said. The city is full of greater opportunities than rural areas or sub-urbs where the sidewalks get rolled up at eight in the evening.

The reason at its most basic is based on math. Where the population density is great-est you have a better chance of meeting people. You may think that you have a lot of friends and don't need a social circle. You are wrong. You need new friends to go with the newly sin-gle you. Friends on the peripheries tend to cy-cle in and out of our lives every so often. Di-vorce provides a harsh break for these languid comings and goings of the friends in life. In any event, the city is the only realistic place for a newly single man. And maybe a new city is a good idea. Why a new city? Because there is no baggage, no running into restaurants or places where you used to go with your ex.

The next question is, where in the city? An anonymous apartment building can be just as bad as living by yourself on a farm in a rural area. All too often we do not know our neighbors. Other than passing people in the halls of your building, have you ever taken the time to get to know them? They could someday save your life. But here we're not interested in life-saving as much as an active social scene.

You are going to have to study to find a place. Take your time. Don't sign any long-term leases and don't buy a place. Sublet or take a month to month. The new friends that you don't have yet will be a fountain of information as to where to go, but you can't ask them. Where do people in the hospitality industry live? In that industry there is usually a high turnover of staff and that means lots of new people and just-vacated apartments. Visit different apartment buildings, but not during the day, except on Saturdays. If the rec rooms look like they are in brand new pristine condition go elsewhere–it means that they are for the most part unused.

For some reason apartment complexes that are spread out horizontally are more welcoming than high rises. Don't ask me why, it's just the case. You want your privacy but you don't want a place that's completely anonymous.

After you find a decent complex, what kind of place should you get? At the beginning, a studio is the wrong call unless cash is an issue. You are working on your social life here, so see if you can afford a two bedroom apartment. Consider a roommate. There is no question but that if you love your privacy–apart from the problem of what to do with your stuff, getting a roommate seems initially to be a horrible idea. But it's not.

CHAPTER 12

Avatars

One bit of advice that you will often hear about dating is the admonition to "Be yourself." This advice is useless. It ignores millions of years of evolution; it ignores our lizard brains and animal selves. Do you really want to be yourself? You can continue staying at home, alone and being yourself all you want. The mating game is a state different from what you are normally accustomed to; we are serially monogamous and hunting a mate requires behavior very different from what is permitted when a mate is found.

This is true in the animal Kingdom as well. As recounted by Neil Strauss in *The Game*, Eric

von Markovic a/k/a "Mystery" described behaviors to attract females. He called this "peacocking" and the peacock is an excellent example from the animal kingdom. The male
peacock extends his glorious fan of feathers
in order to obtain the attention of females.
Eric recommended behavior bordering on the
outrageous, but it is not necessary to resort
to extremes. Maybe a pair of expensive or
expensive-looking shoes or a sport coat is
enough.

The essential lesson, though, is a good one.
You cannot be yourself. You have to be someone special, someone with energy, someone
who is confident and attractive. This is not an
issue of looks, for as we learned in an earlier
chapter, attraction is not a choice. But that
doesn't mean that you be sloppy or let yourself
go.

There is nothing wrong with trying to attract a partner and to do so you simply cannot
be yourself. You can bring out another facet of
your own personality, but you simply cannot

be yourself unless you are completely content with the way things are going on the girlfriend front. And if you are completely satisfied, then you're probably not reading this book anyway.

Instead of being yourself, re-invent yourself and at least be able to step out into that character each time you go out sarging. This is a skill, not unlike acting. As you practice you will get better. Soon it will become second nature and you will wonder why everything was once so difficult and why you wasted so much time sitting on a bar stool by yourself. Nevertheless, your peacocking personality has to be an extension of the person you already are. Otherwise you won't be able to pull it off; it will seem fake. It has to be you but it is not you at the same time.

My work colleague Florian always wore a tie. Whenever he went out he was overwhelmed. There were people having fun but he wasn't one of them. He didn't know what to do. He was shy, nervous. He couldn't get a girlfriend. I told him to play to his strengths.

"You're balding, forget the combover. Consider shaving your head. Get a leather jacket and mack out as a Bulgarian gangster." Florian was far from being a Bulgarian gangster. But he knew that he couldn't just "be himself" either. Something had to change. If you think you need to make a change, you do.

CHAPTER 13

On Line

According to the National Academy of Sciences, a little more than one-third of recent new marriages began on-line. One of the biggest mistakes that you can make when using Internet dating services or places like Craigslist is spending too much time on-line. I cannot emphasize this enough. The on-line world is not the real world. There is no reason why you can't set up a meeting on-line, but that should be your purpose. Get on-line, find a possible candidate(s), set up a meeting, and get off the computer. Endless texting back and forth is a waste of time. It is too likely that there will be misunderstandings because of the nature of a text, which is somewhere between a conversation and writing.

The danger of on-line introductions is staying on-line too long. Chatting or texting with a stranger over a period of weeks is not productive. This is a huge mistake. Conversational e-mails are easily misconstrued. This is especially perilous given the dating context. Flirting on-line often comes across as creepiness.

You will never get laid on-line, so you have to take it off-line as soon as possible. As soon as you can, exchange phone numbers and agree to meet. Set up the meet for a public place, preferably during daylight, at a place where there will be a lot of people around. Remember at this stage you are a stranger and presumed dangerous until proven otherwise.

Don't expect or offer a full date. A meeting of no more than an hour–an informal non-threatening semi-speed date at a coffee shop–will give you both the chance to decide whether it's worthwhile to meet again.

While the rules are different for texts, it

is still all too easy to unintentionally offend. If you are talking to someone and you see that you have been misunderstood or stepped over the line you can gauge their reaction and immediately apologize or provide an explanation. That cannot happen with a text. The nature of the medium is that though the words are exchanged in a conversational context they are nevertheless written and the written word is different. While it can be explained, it cannot be denied. An idle comment will come back to haunt you. You will not be able to deny that you said it and it is difficult to take back anything that is there in black and white on the page or screen.

After you have set up a meeting; after you have had sex, then you can spend time texting as long as you follow the rules for phone conversations. The point is not the content. Always keep it light. Focus on the next meeting always.

Texts can be useful because they can sop up some of that new relationship energy. Girls–

and some men–love them and waste time texting all day. If your new friend starts sending you texts you can't ignore them. But don't fall into the trap of replying immediately. Send one reply for every two or three of hers. If you reply immediately to every text you let her know that she can command you or that you are glued to the alternate reality of the Internet and are a slave to its commands.

The pattern set at the beginning of a relationship tends to persist throughout. If she has gotten used to your immediate responses to her texts, she will be suspicious when all of a sudden you do not reply immediately. Are you with another woman? Is your relationship an exclusive one? Maybe it is time to have "the" conversation.

Let her know that you are not glued to your cell phone or the computer terminal. Let her know that there will be times when you won't answer. Sometimes, especially late in the evening, it is best to let the text go by and wait till the next day to respond. Or respond with a contentless call. Or something silly about a current event, meme, what's on YouTube or in the news.

Tell her this in person. Writing will come off as just a little bit too harsh. And that is another reason why you have to shy away from too much texting.

There is no reason why you shouldn't take a look at online dating services. Some people say that there is a stigma attached, but in this day of technological overrun I don't see how that is still the case. We seem to find everything else on-line, why not a mate? One advantage of on-line dating is that your search can fit your schedule. More importantly, women use on-line services. More importantly still, the male/female ratio on-line is more favorable for older guys in comparison to younger men. That is, there are fewer eligible men on-line as people age. Twenty-something women who set up profiles on popular sites will get dozens of responses. A guy in his twenties will get few, if any. By the time you reach your fifties you will get many more responses than if you were younger. There are many more available women than men in our demographic. Some of these will come from women you would like to meet.

I am not going to suggest one service over another. They all tend to come and go. You probably have heard of some of them and new ones are springing up all the time. Match.com, okcupid and plentyoffish are all possibilities. There are ethnically-oriented sites. J-Date, if you're Jewish; muslima dot com for Muslims– and even anti-diversity sites such as American Singles. Exclusionary is not a word that should be in your vocabulary. At this stage you're home alone. You may find that special someone coming from a background that you hadn't previously considered.

Absolutely stay away from any site promising free NSA sex. Adult Friend Finder is a waste of time. I have never met anyone, not even the cousin of a friend of a friend of a friend–who has had any luck on such sites.

There are no sexually frustrated college girls dying to meet older men on these sites.

E-Harmony demands a large investment of time in order to complete a seemingly endless questionnaire, but you will get dates. Events and Adventures calls themselves an "activity club." For a fee, they sponsor singles events in your city. They seem to have more female than male members. This could be a good thing. One member I interviewed told me that he just was too tired to organize a social life and that E & A always had something going on.

Because the barrier to entry is nonexistent free sites have more listings than paid sites. Many candidates are not all that serious about dating. They admit that a girlfriend or their children got them to put up a profile. The picture is usually taken with a phone with the flash setting on "high", some guy has been cropped out of the picture–or worse, he's still in–and the profile makes it obvious that woman isn't serious.

When you are writing a profile you are writing advertising copy. Give the effort a certain amount of thought. If you don't advertise you won't sell.

Your picture should look like you and be no more than five years old. Otherwise the woman you meet on-line will feel immediately deceived when she meets you in person. Starting a relationship off on the wrong foot is a terrible idea. It is very hard to analyze yourself. Looking in the mirror isn't easy. A profile is not a resumé. This is dating, the process is supposed to be fun. The goal should be a combo of honesty and humor.

You don't have much experience writing these profiles, but by this time in your life you've sold more than one car and you've read dozens of car ads. So if all else fails, write a car ad. Write a profile trying to sell yourself as if you were a new car. New battery, minor wear and tear, high mileage but air blows cold. Whatever you think is important that you would put in a car ad. If you can't do this, pull a car ad from the paper and use it as your profile. "Low mileage late model for sale. Hobbies: 4 new tires. Air blows ice cold. Call for a test drive" It sounds silly, but at some level it's amusing, it's fun and it helps you get words on paper. Of course, your mileage may vary.

Or if you would prefer, write a sincere, emo-art student profile channeling your inner sixteen year old. The beauty of on-line dating is that you will still get a few responses.

CHAPTER 14

Younger women

A man, though his hair be gray, can always get a wife, but a woman's time is short.
–Theophilus

Tengo could not quite relax when he was with energetic young college girls. It was like playing with a kitten, fresh and fun at first, but tiring in the end.

–Murakami, Haruki (2011-10-25). *1Q84* (Kindle Locations 1169-1170). Random House, Inc.. Kindle Edition.

Old bulls prefer tender grass.

−Chinese proverb

An old man had a girlfriend fifty years younger. His friend asked him about the final reality that stalks us all. "And in time, what will happen?" The old man was nonplussed. "If she dies, she dies."

This is an old joke but contains some useful wisdom. Relationships don't last that long anyway. They say that love lasts three years. If you have three years to give, you should not feel guilty about the age difference. There isn't much of a real long run anymore. Thirty year marriages are rare. Relationships are lucky to survive a year. If you've got three years to give, you can give a whole relationship. If you have a girlfriend for three or six months, your age is, as is hers. It may be the reason why you eventually break up but hopefully it will be fun for both of you while it lasts. Don't start worrying about what things are going to be like when you are much older−that day may never, ever come. Don't worry about age. There are other things to worry about, but this isn't one of them.

Beauty is fleeting.

It is unfair, but women seem to age faster than men. We seem to be able to maintain our looks for a decade longer. As you get older, the statistics change. According to the web dating site OKCupid.com, older single men are in great demand–there simply aren't enough of us. Cruise ship lines have been known to hire age appropriate men as live-aboards to entertain older women on cruises. And then there are the younger women who are interested in older men.

There are lots of well-known celebrity examples. Paul McCartney. Anthony Quinn. Michael Douglas. Celine Dion. Charlie Chaplin. Rupert Murdoch. There are some less famous. 83 year old Gaston Glock, maker of the 16 shot eponymous handgun and his new wife, Kathrin Tschikof, who is in her early 30's. Yoani Sanchez, the Cuban blogger who is the darling of Miami's Cuban exile community, met her husband when she was 17. At the time, he was 47. At the age of 68, the Japanese poet Jan Kamada stole the wife of one of his disciples. He then had the good fortune to give her two children and to live another twenty years.

In the animal world we might learn from our closest relative. The silver-backed chimpanzee mates with the young females of his troop. One of my friends swears that these behaviors naturally come to humans and that young women are programmed to seek out older men.

There is even a web site where younger women who are into older men can share their stories: earnthenecklace dot com. These women are not gold-diggers and they claim that their relationships must be taken seriously. Since many of these relationships eventually led to marriage, it's hard to argue. Still, it's easy to see the anguish experienced by these women when even their friends laugh about their marrying an antique. "My husband's age is no joke," one writes. People can be envious of happiness. While these relationships have been common throughout history, expect that there will be sniping from the peanut gallery by both jealous men and women.

Assume younger women cheat. If you want them not to lie to you, stop asking questions about what they're doing and who they're doing it with.

In the long run, a relationship with a younger woman won't work. The external life that surrounds her, work, school, will be so different from yours that it is like a foreign language that you will never learn to speak, a cultural barrier that you can never cross and which will make communication difficult or tedious. That is not to say that you can't find shared interests. Music. Photography. Technology. Politics. News. And in the long run there is no long run.

The other insight that I hope is useful has to do with the older man/younger women dynamic. There has been much written about this subject: how the "perfect" age for a woman is half your age plus seven.

Men of all ages are attracted to younger women. But relatively few young women are interested in older men. Nevertheless, a certain percentage of young women are generally attracted to and prefer older men. In other words, for a certain percentage the dynamic is one of true reciprocal interest.

I wasn't sure what to make of this. I have heard girls in their twenties complain about the lack of maturity in boys their age, but the nature of their complaints made it clear that that young men in their twenties did not lack maturity. For the most part, they were acting like men do. The girls complained that the men did not take them seriously, that they did not want to commit, that they hopped from one girlfriend to the other. These are complaints that are just as valid at age fifty as they are at twenty.

There was one class of complaint that seemed to be more genuine and had more to do with where these young guys were in life. Many did not have jobs or still lived with their parents. They did not own an automobile nor really have any desire to obtain one. The girls had financial needs that young guys simply had no way of meeting. You can look at this as pure meretriciousness and say that these women only cared about money but I don't think that is the whole story.

In dating, it is important to play to your strengths. There is absolutely nothing wrong in doing so. You will not be able to compete against a guy in his twenties in terms of strength, stamina or even just staying out late. You may be able to keep pace for a while, but you won't be able to with any consistency. If you compete at this level, you will lose.

There is a story about a young woman who was a contestant on a Chinese dating program and who selected an average-looking, but wealthy older man over several much younger handsome candidates. When asked why she said that she would "rather cry in the back seat of a BMW than smile while riding a bicycle."

If you can play the financially secure card, why not? You may feel that it's all about money. It's not. Money, position and maturity are part of what you are. Why pretend that these qualities don't exist? Instead, embrace them and capitalize on them. Open the door to the BMW so the young lady can get in.

Still, this didn't seem to explain the whole story. Some of these young girls boasted about their older boyfriends who were anything but financially secure. They lived not in Mcmansions but otherwise nondescript apartments. BMW's weren't in the picture.

So what was going on?

The younger woman/older man dynamic is a sexual preference just like any other. Some younger women are attracted to older men. They find our age and maturity attractive in the same way that you might prefer brunettes to blondes or are keenly interested in a particular body part. There are Cuban guys in Miami who just love those big booty gals from Hialeah and who don't pay a hell of a lot of attention to their chests. These preferences are hard-wired. Because they are fixed there is no way to change them. I either like blonde girls or I don't. If I don't, nothing is really going to change that. I have nothing against blonde girls, but just speaking for me, if there's a hot blonde standing to the left of a hot brunette I'll take the door on the right. Every time.

In the same way, a girl who has this preference is going to be attracted to older guys no matter what, even if she tells her girlfriends that older guys are creepy and eww.

What is "older" is often a question of degree. An 18-year old who has just graduated from high school will find a man in his 30's ancient. Four years later that age difference will be manageable but guys in their 40's may be a stretch. How do you tell which girls are interested in older men and which are not?

The fact that she is much younger than you and is still talking to you after you've flirted with her a little bit is a pretty good sign.

And if she walks away? Don't feel bad about it. A sexual preference is one of the components of attraction. Attraction is either there or it isn't. If it's not, don't feel bad. It's not about you personally. But understanding that this is a sexual preference makes what would otherwise be a rejection more tolerable.

The first time I slept with a young girl I felt terrible. She was younger than my daughter and thirty years separated her from my 50. I felt guilty, horrible. I was a monster, a dirty old man preying on young women. I thought that she was in her late twenties when in fact she was just twenty. An honest mistake. She really liked older men. I asked her why but this is a silly question. No one knows the "why" to such questions, they simply are the way that they are. She guessed that it was because boys her age didn't have jobs, weren't established, didn't know how to take charge. But it was really none of that–she simply liked older men.

I called up a friend to commiserate. You

won't believe what I've just done. I told him. I told him I felt guilty. My rabbi had always listened to my sins and never let me down, even though I'm not Jewish.

It was like that scene in The Godfather where the Don slaps Johnny Fontane across the face and mocks his tears. Who the fuck do you think you are? You feel guilty? God just gave you a gift. Who are you to spit in his eye and turn his gift down? Just who do you think you are?

The second time the guilt had almost all gone away. Guilt is like that. The best way to get rid of it is to repeat whatever made you feel guilty in the first place. Some younger girls prefer older men. So what? There is nothing else that you need to know.

CHAPTER 15

Older Women

By "older women" I am referring to women your age or just a bit younger. It never ceases to amaze me how a guy without a date will overlook hot, eligible and attractive women to chase fruitlessly after a girl twenty years younger who is simply not into older men.

Older women are still girls.

They sext. They are playful. They write letters. They are fun and sophisticated and well worth your time.

There are two kinds of older women. There are those who have let themselves go and those who have fought aging every step of the way. Those who have let themselves go are not in the game. If they go out it's almost accidental. I am not going to spend much time discussing them because you will know who they are instantly. They have let themselves go because they were secure in their lives and their needs were met and so, why bother? You probably were the same way at the midpoint of your last marriage. There you are at the barbecue–why not grab another pork rib? And don't forget to ask the waiter to bring more bread sticks after you've finished the basket that was on the table.

Older women can be absolutely exquisite. They are beautiful, playful and wise. They are comfortable with their bodies, secure in their skin. They know what those bodies are capable of, what they can and cannot do. They are just as adventurous as younger girls. A younger girl may or may not want glamour shots, but you will find that the older gal is the one who brings up the subject and loses no time in losing her clothes and pulling a fur coat out of the closet. When it comes to sex they are shameless. They learned long ago how to deep throat a cock without gagging and take delight in their skill. Just try to find a younger girl with the same skill set. Older gals are up for anything. If you mention a kinky fantasy she'll start planning how she can make it happen. But why wait? What's wrong with now?

It's strange–with over 10 million copies sold I have had some difficulty finding a woman who admits to having read Fifty Shades of Grey. At a party once, every woman in attendance denied reading it until one admitted that her mother had read it and that she might have looked when her mother wasn't reading and then the dam broke and all of them admitted they had lied. They all had read the book.

When you're sitting with one of these lying older women who mentions the subject, have no doubt that she will run off and bring back scarves herself for you to tie her up.

Older women are courtesans who mastered the art of conversation long ago. They are up to date on politics and current events. The references you make will be understood and not met with quizzical looks If they don't really care about your job or your problems at work they will make you think that they do. They like the finer things in life; and while from time to time they may agree to rough it with you at a campsite you will soon learn that this isn't really what they are all about. They may have a condo or a house that they won in a divorce. They will be more financially secure than the twenty-something whose credit cards are maxed out and who doesn't have money for a taxicab.

From time to time she may pick up the check when you go out. She will invite you. If she insists on paying, let her do so. It's because she wants to. This is one of the ways that she wants to show that she cares for you, so from time to time let her. This is the exception and not the rule. You are much more likely to find that an older gal prefers traditional dating roles with the man picking up the check. Don't forget to follow up with a nice gift.

Older women are faced with the same issues that we have. They don't know where to go to meet men. They don't want to run through one meaningless date after another to find a nice guy. They want a nice guy but like all women they don't. They don't mind going to night clubs every now and then but feel threatened by all the twenty-somethings there.

Like us, they welcome the attentions of those younger. The attention given in the media to cougars gave many older women new hope. If you find yourself chasing after an older woman who seems to have a circle of younger boyfriends, from time to time she may want to spend time with an older gentleman. That individual might be you.

An older woman is not going to complain if you don't want to stay out until four in the morning or even if you say "let's call it a night" after a hard day at work. The cliché is that older women are more understanding, but all this means is that an older woman has had more life experiences.

The other cliché is that older women are more grateful. This is pretty conceited. Exquisite older gals have no problem finding boyfriends and after you have been dumped for a guy in his 70's, you're standing there wondering what the hell just happened? So don't think that you are God's gift to a woman just because she's fifty like you.

The exquisite older woman is a precious resource too often overlooked by us fifty-somethings new to the dating scene. You make a grievous error by excluding them.

There are only two potential downsides to dating an older woman. The first is the problem of mixing worlds. Because of her age and independence she will have a life in the way that a twenty or thirty-something will not. You may not fit into that life. Her friends will be protective and they may not like you. You may find that you don't like them either.

You may know nothing about her professional career and you may not fit in well there. She may take you to parties where people presume that you are in the same field or share their same interests and will be surprised or shun you if you don't. The advantage of the older woman in these circumstances is that she knows how to carve out a space in her life that the two of you can inhabit. She knows that from time to time it has to be about you and all about you and that your really could give two shits about classical music.

The second is breaking up. Like us, older women know that the end of the path is closer than we think. They seem to take break-ups so much harder than a younger woman. A younger woman may think that because she has always enjoyed the attention of men that there will be another guy around the corner. An older woman has the experience to know that this is not always true.

The worst break-up of my life resulted in a stalker. On one occasion she snuck into my garage and shredded a garden hose. I'm still not sure how she did it. She called the police and reported me missing. She reached

my aged parents and did the same thing–
obviously my not calling for her meant that I
must have been disappeared by a right-wing
death squad. How she got my parents' number is beyond me, since I never told her their
names, they live in a different state and don't
have a computer.

The other break-up resulted in me being
shunned by those whom I thought were my
friends. She told them that I had driven her to
a dangerous drawbridge, made her get out and
urged her to jump off if she was really so dis-
traught that I was breaking up with her. They
looked at me as if I was a murderer. The truth
is I walked out on her at a bar because, well, it
was over, and she followed me to a city bridge
that I had to walk over to get back to my car.
Fortunately, her friends were aware of her talent for exaggeration after she asked me to stay
friends and invited me to her house for parties
and occasional NSA adventures.

CHAPTER 16

Married Women

Dating a married woman is playing with fire. If you want real adventure in an otherwise risk-free life, start dating a married woman. There are some advantages–sex is on the table right away in a way that it simply is not with a single woman. If her needs were being met at home she would not be talking to you. She may not admit this because she may not realize it herself.

If you want a relationship that is similar to a cloak and dagger operation, full of lies and betrayals, where you live in the moment or not at all, then by all means, have at it.

Once these kind of relationships were made of pay phones, calls that end in a hang-up when the wrong person answered, lunchtime meetings in far away places and wandering around in a public square and wondering if you should leave because she hasn't shown up yet. Something might have happened with her family. The plans you make will be cancelled at the last minute without any explanation whatsoever.

New technology brings new problems. Everyone has a cell phone so now you can call or text to find out why she is late or if she is coming at all. The answer won't necessarily be the truth, but it doesn't matter. The problem with lying is trying to keep all of the various stories straight in your head. She has to lie to you, to her husband, to her friends. Even experienced liars make mistakes. She will make them. The only question is how bad will the fall-out be?

Additionally, now you have to worry about the creation of records sent–those cell phone calls and logs are evidence. Incriminating information hides deep within file systems and the Cloud. Those texts are witnesses and erasing them is not easy. Even if she erases everything on the phone there are back-ups, there are records the cell phone companies made, there are e-mails and other evidence hiding on the hard drive in /tmp directories that you didn't realize existed before, not to mention NSA intercepts that supposedly no one is reading.

If you think that all this is fantasy and can't happen you have never sat in a dark room with a frightened girl hoping that the process server will quit banging on the door and go away and you have never seen the results of a subpoena detailing the existence of calls to a number you claimed wasn't yours.

Every relationship has its ups and downs. However the relationship between you and your married girlfriend is going, add to the recipe a beaker of guilt and things become even more complicated. Is she upset with you or with herself? Today she wants to see you but there is no way that she is going to be able to get out of the house by herself. To do she will have to lie to her children for you. This is a very long bridge to cross. She will ask herself if you are worth it.

There are, of course, exceptions to the rule. Some women are starting to treat one or two year old marriages as "starter marriages" which really don't count and can be walked away from without much worry. Both parties go their own way just like you stopped going steady when you were fifteen and no one worries about it.

It will be hard to be the alpha male in this kind of relationship because so much needs to be kept secret. You have to let the wants and desires of others take precedence over your own because she belonged to them first. If she starts talking about leaving her husband for you then you know you are in deep trouble indeed. For her it will be out of the frying pan into the fire. You will always think that if she cheated once on someone else, she can cheat again, but this time on you.

The other thing to think about is that the

emotionally distant, cold, alcoholic and abusive husband is probably just a guy like you. Whatever faults he has have been exaggerated horribly to help her live with herself and to rationalize her cheating. The danger is when you start to think that your relationship with your married girlfriend is going to be the exception. When people are told they have a 95% chance of dying they imagine immediately that they are in the 5%. They are not. You are not in the 5%.

So if a hot woman tell you she is separated, remember Ronald Reagan's sage advice: trust, but verify.

CHAPTER **17**

Brisket Brigade

What is the brisket brigade? The term refers to the lonely widows who will show up on your doorstep after your own partner dies to console you. I first learned about this secret army while visiting a friend in Century Village, where the average age is about 70. He pointed out that the brigade's tactics never varied. The come-on is irresistible. You are emotionally weak. Alone. You haven't eaten. You haven't given any thought to eating. Next thing you know there's an attractive female at your door, a friend of a friend, someone safe. It's not dating. She is bearing food. You let her in. The place is a mess. This hasn't been done and that hasn't been done. She offers to pitch in. Before you know it you have a new partner.

When I first heard the term I thought that it only applied to widowers in their 70's–or beyond–but then I realized that in a less noticeable way the brigade engages in maneuvers involving much younger men, men in their 50's, like you. So don't be surprised that after word gets around about your divorce, or the fact that you are alone, that unattached women in the neighborhood start to show up without an invitation, bearing gifts. Welcome them. If someone has taken the time to make you a casserole, she is interested in you enough to date you. She may even have been interested in you for a while. So who are you to ignore her genuine interest?

CHAPTER 18

No Fear

William Faulkner's novella, *Wild Palms*, is about a Chicago gangster on the run with his girlfriend in Hot Springs, Arkansas. The chapters of the story alternate with a completely unrelated tale because the editor thought that the story was too intense–and novellas unpublishable. So they coupled two novellas together, alternating chapter by chapter. This is a useful technique. The lesson here is push-pull. You can't be serious all of the time. You have to be serious some of the time. But you can't always be intense. It's tedious. You have to drop out of seriousness with its opposite: humor. Humor lets you float ideas without being responsible for them. Talk about a threesome. "It was a joke." Talk about her spending the night. "Haha I was just flirting." It's a good way to gauge reactions.

David D'Angelo calls this cocky-funny. It works in bars where you need to show that you are an alpha male. But cockiness, egotism and conceitedness gets very tiresome quickly. You are not that wonderful. A person who believes himself to be God's gift to women is most assuredly not. The line between a conceited person and an asshole is a thin one. Maybe there isn't a boundary at all. You may have a great job and a bankroll and be financially secure, but there is always someone who has more. There is always someone who is better in some way.

Relationships with women are push/pull. You push. You pull. You are serious. You are not. You like her. You show indifference. You keep her on her toes. Some couples are afraid of marriage because they don't want to lose this edge. These things keep a relationship at any stage new and alive. The enemy of passion is complacency. Falling into familiar patterns will mean the death of love. The opposite of love isn't hate. The opposite of love is indifference.

Follow-up anything serious you might say with a little humor.

Perhaps the most significant and liberating insight comes from David D'Angelo. I can take no credit for it, but it is perhaps the foundation of successful game at 50 or any other age. D'Angelo's insight is that attraction is not a choice. This insight is sublime. Great ideas are often simple and obvious after discovery. D'Angelo's insight is an significant contribution. Both simple and obvious, the realization is astonishing and its consequence even more so. If attraction is a choice, there is no rejection.

Either attraction is there, or it isn't. If it isn't there, don't take it personally. It's not about you, it's not a rejection of your self or your personality or your feelings or the way you look. It is merely a statement of scientific fact: there is no attraction. If the other person is not attracted to you they have not rejected you. The attraction simply isn't there. Walk away. You haven't been rejected–you merely hold a piece from a different puzzle than the one she's putting together. There is no shame in this.

Fear of rejection is what holds us back. The recognition that attraction is not a choice frees us from rejection. You don't want to approach the hot, available woman because you are afraid she will tell you to get lost. The fear of rejection burns. But if she says no, what has she really said? All she has said is that for her, the attraction isn't there. She can't decide to be attracted to you–it is as impossible for her as it is for you to be attracted to blondes when you prefer brunettes. That is all it means, nothing more. Once you realize this, you can never be rejected again. Never. That is empowering. Now you can introduce yourself to anyone without fear, for you cannot be rejected.

Shyness has a direct correlation to the fear of rejection. You will find that once you understand and integrate the absence of rejection, any shyness you might have had will disappear as well.

Rejection can only come later in a relationship, when a woman who was first attracted to you has gotten to know you and for whatever reason has decided to break it off. That rejection does hurt, precisely because the person who was once attracted to you and who came to know you no longer wants you. You can feel bad about that. But this book is about meeting new people and making new friends. In that context, D'Angelo is right: there is no such thing as rejection.

CHAPTER **19**

Places

Everyone seems to have their own opinion about where to go to meet women. Each town and most neighborhoods will have recommended or known places. There is probably a cool place in your town, but keep in mind that a place is made by the people who frequent it. Otherwise, just about every bar is the same.

Pundits who claim you can meet women "anywhere" are not being helpful. Sure, lightning can strike whenever, but otherwise there is a time and a place. If a woman gets dressed up to go out and meet new people she has invested time and money in her appearance: she wants to be approached. A woman who ran out to the store in a t-shirt, pajama bottoms and flip flops to buy milk or cigarets probably isn't thinking about being chatted up. So leave her alone.

Other than bars, nightclubs and restaurants, there are few reliable places.

As you get older, there are fewer and fewer types of non-family events where you can expect to meet people. You may find it difficult finding mixers designed for the over-50's but there may be a few around. Softball, golf or bowling leagues can be a good bet. Organized card games as well. Women seem to let their hair down at weddings. Any kind of political event. Gallery openings. Fundraisers for a cause. Food-oriented events. In Miami there is an event called "Feast with the Beasts" where a group of young professionals try new recipes from local restaurants and run amok in the zoo after hours. Charity runs.

What would Ovid suggest? His concrete suggestion was to go to gladiator games. Unfortunately, that is no longer possible. But what about Nascar? Professional tennis? There's no point in traipsing up and down a golf course if you're not going to play, but the corporate tents and parties are another story. Lots of different people come to play, and not necessarily golf. Trade shows, seminars, festivals and events are all possibilities.

Dinner and a movie–these places are for a date, not to find a person to take on a date. There is no point in reviewing movie listings, except to know what's out there so that if the topic of conversation comes up you will have some idea of what people are talking about.

Nightclubs–there is only one thing you have to take to a nightclub. Bring energy. For the entire time you are there. That means dancing, running around, making contacts with different people. The action starts at midnight so it helps if you are a vampire. If you started drinking at 8:00 in the evening you're in serious trouble. Plan how you are going to get home before you go and get ready for the aches and pains the next morning.

It will be fun, a lot of fun. But even if it's not, there is enough eye candy and such a buzz that the next morning you'll say to yourself, "I'm glad I went." It's just that you won't be planning any trips back anytime soon.

Take advantage of your bartenders. They are not merely beverage preparers. Instead, think of them as networking professionals. Not true? What do you think your bartender knows about you? Where you work, how often you come in, or maybe just that you're a new face. Maybe they've heard someone say something about you. Multiply this by the number of people who come into the place and what you really have is the hub of a wheel connecting all the spokes on the seats.

Having the bartender introduce you to someone in his or her bar is a great improvement over an anonymous approach because it takes you out of the stranger zone and puts you into the category of "friend of a friend." There's always some feeling, however well hidden, that a stranger harbors trouble or threats. But friends of friends are not in that category. So bartenders can lubricate social interaction in a way far beyond just pouring drinks. From time to time a female bartender may surprise you and ask, "why don't you ask me out?" Such requests must be given careful consideration because if you like the bar and break-up with the bartender, you've lost both.

So be sure to use their skills. And don't forget to tip generously.

Think twice about staying out all night. Do you really want to meet a woman who hangs out in nightclubs till four in the morning? Normally at 4 am you are in bed sound asleep but if you're in a relationship with a party girl club kid you will be wide awake wondering where she is or dragging yourself yet again into the forest to watch the nocturnal animals. Forget about plans for the morning–people who are still up at 4 am can't reliably get to work by 9:00. So this has to be at best an occasional venue, nothing more.

In Paris night clubs are opening earlier in order to cater to the older set. In Miami, tea dances on Sundays have long been a part of the South Beach scene. If you believe that "nothing good happens after midnight" check out scenes like these. If this movement catches on, there will be new scenes to explore without worrying about the productivity hit when you stay out till four or five a.m.

There are places that are structured for meeting people and there are places where people simply happen to congregate for a purpose other than interaction. The first category consists of bars, wine tastings and events of different kinds. In the latter category there are shopping malls, grocery stores and other places where people must go in order to purchase the necessities of life. Will you meet people in a grocery store? You can, but grocery stores are not for meeting people. If can happen, but it's unlikely.

There are places that pretend to be for one purpose but that purpose is often a clever mask for their real purpose, which is bringing people together. Adult education classes are a good example of this. Maybe you really want to learn how to speak Italian. At least you can pretend, as does everyone else, that is the real reason for signing up.

Take advantage of continuing education in a field you are interested in or one you have always wanted to learn more about, whether it's photography, how to set up equations in an Excel spreadsheet or how to change the oil in your car. One of the advantages of this "back to school" concept is that, just like when you were in college, there will be a group with shared interests interested in social action. And yes, some women are there for the same reason you are. Keep telling yourself that you really, really want to speak Italian and the fact you've seen a few cute women sign up for the course has nothing to do with it.

Of course it doesn't.

If you want an educational experience without the commitment, colleges and other institutions, such as the Council on Foreign Relations, sponsor lectures on a wide variety of subjects. These are often barely masked social mixers. Chambers of Commerce, business and trade organizations often sponsor lectures as well.

Don't be afraid of going outside your comfort zone. Nascar may not be for you, but it may not be for the woman you meet there either. Both of you may be there for reasons other than the race. In sum, any place where strangers might interact is a good place to meet new people. Or maybe you need go no further than your local corner saloon. You need to do research to find a place that's appropriate for you. The venues are out there.

You don't want to go to bars anymore, and besides, there are a lot of women who are tired of the bar scene. Nightclubs take too much effort, the crowd is consistently too young and your next day will always take a productivity hit.

One of the reasons why you open a book

like this is because you hope that it contains the recipe for the secret sauce which will make it possible for you to meet new women consistently. As part of that, you expect to find a list of places to go and hope that there are one or two places on the list that you haven't considered.

I have never seen as much outright, overt hooking up as I have at national political conventions. This doesn't start at the national level and happen once every four years. It happens all the time. So this isn't advice about one physical place, but an avocation which will bring so many benefits: politics.

Organized political groups are not called parties idly. Parties are a principal way for people in the party to get together and interact. Whether you call these parties fundraisers, or get to know the candidates, or dinners, they are in fact parties. And you are invited. It takes very little to get active with your local political group. Americans have a genius for overlapping jurisdictions, so the larger town you live in the more opportunities you will find for political shindigs. Volunteer–sometimes this can be as simple as showing up for an event–and next thing you know you are invited to one event after another.

You will have something in common with women at these events. You both have an excuse to be there, you both have something to talk about after introducing yourself–though nametags are often de rigeur at political events. Choose a party whose principles you can at least tolerate and you're good to go. If you can't stomach either (or any of them) choose a cause and get involved with the cause, or pick the party that's most sympathetic to the cause. It really doesn't matter. If you can't stomach politics at all, try a charity.

People at these events are there to say to meet and greet the candidate, but when that's over they are ready to have fun. Often there's an open bar. You would be surprised how many political events there are. There are events for candidates, for the party, for causes.

There are judicial get togethers where you can say hello to one or more of the hundreds of faceless wannabe judges looking for a campaign contribution.

There are local, state and federal candidates for hundreds of positions. There are flyers to hand out, posters to post, donated beer to taste (at the convention I attended it was Budweiser).

While you will find dozens of enthusiastic and energetic young people at political events, the crowd tends to trend older. This is because politics is ultimately all about money and older people tend to have more money than younger people. If people think you have money–whether you do or not–they will invite you to events in the hope that you will contribute.

In addition to politics, the art world is particularly geared towards meeting new people–people who, ultimately will buy art. Gallery opening nights have to be filled and it's not that difficult to get on the lists. Some cities have gallery nights where the galleries all get together, serve wine and it's like one long pub crawl. These are friendly venues where there is something for shy people to talk about–the art hanging on the wall. There may not be much of a collector's scene in your town other than E-bay–but if it exists it will trend older as well. Art Basel is an annual event in Miami which has been called "spring break for the art world." Anyone can attend.

CHAPTER 20

Best Pick-up Line

I was at the Globe when Marta showed up. It was a Wednesday night. This is hardly prime going-out night, but in some cities you will find places that have rather all-out midweek breaks. These tend to come and go. The floating world is fickle and can move quickly from one place to the next apparently without rhyme or reason.

In many cities there are party organizers who can promise bars that they will bring in 20 or so good looking model-types to seed a scene. Word of mouth travels quickly, others want to find out what's happening and the next thing you know there are more than a hundred people spilling out onto the sidewalk and a police cruiser nearby to curb the troublemakers.

In Miami there were at least two such scenes on Wednesday nights. One was at the Globe. The Globe had obtained permission from the city to set up an outside bar on the sidewalk to handle the overflow. Hiring one or two off-duty Coral Gables policemen didn't hurt the zoning modification application either.

The scene consisted of two shifts. The first shift was full of after-work office types; starting around five and finishing no later than eight. The Globe should have given everyone time cards so they could punch in and out. The second shift was made up of people from all over the county; starting at 8 and finishing at 12. After midnight, there was a new scene at the Hyatt, with dancing till two in the morning. Needless to say, some office workers put in three shifts. The idea was to meet someone at the Globe around 8 and then go off to the Hyatt for dancing and getting to know one another a little better.

This kind of a structure is interesting, because when you leave with someone and go to a different venue under circumstances like these it's in effect a second date. The beauty of this kind of set-up is that you don't have to spend an awkward couple of hours over an expensive dinner plate being interviewed–or doing the interviewing–and trying to figure out if you are wasting your time.

At a bar, no one is going to care if you excuse yourself from a conversation, or walk away, or extricate yourself and just leave. That is the nature of public drinking. The worst thing that will happen is that the next day someone might call and ask, "hey, what happened to you?" But probably they won't, because at these places, no one is paying attention. More specifically, no one is paying attention to you. And no one cares.

It took me a long time to realize that any arrangements, promises, undertakings, business deals or political commitments entered into while drinking at a bar are non-binding. You can't hold anyone to their promises or to their claims. A day at the beach planned for the next day at 11 pm after the third rum and coke with someone you just met may or may not happen. You had best call in advance before loading the SUV with the beach chairs. "Oh, I'm sorry, I forgot I had my Pilates class" and that's that.

Making extraordinary claims about yourself—"I am Hillary Clinton's brother," for example—is probably a bad idea unless the claim is true. The most outlandish claims are however, paradoxically the ones most likely to be true while the little exaggerations are more likely to be false. Someone claiming to be a "police sergeant" is probably just a mall security guard while Hillary's brother, Hugh Rodman, in fact does live in Coral Gables and from time to time is seen around town.

So on one occasion, I was outside talking to Catherine, my favorite bartender, when Marta came in. She was wearing a white dress and was all made up. Marta is a schoolteacher, but she had not been wearing that dress in the classroom and her students had never seen her wearing that shade of red lipstick.

She ordered a vodka and tonic and stood around the outdoor bar. If she was with friends I didn't see them. The women congregated with other women, leaving the men to hang out with each other. This was not a strict separation–it just seemed that one side was predominantly women, while the other side was predominantly men. I had seen this kind of separation before–but where? Then I remembered. Middle school dances. Boys and girls kept to their own gender because the opposite sex consisted of strange creatures and no one really knew what to do with the other.

Marta was a friend of a friend. She saw me and came over. "Why won't anybody talk to me?" she asked. "I got all dressed up! What's the matter with these guys?"

Men agonize over killer pick-up lines. We've all heard them, from the clever to the profane. We look for them in books, on the Internet and try to get them from our friends. Admit it–not a few of you have picked up this book and are thumbing through it RIGHT NOW and turning to this chapter just to get the best pick-up line. So we've all read these witty, useless lines. Most of them are a little bit sexual–some of them are a lot sexual–and you think that the line will cast a magic spell which will hypnotize your new friend and convince her to come home with you.

Learning pick-up lines and their delivery is great if you are going to do stand-up comedy. Or if you've been doing it all your life.

You're not doing stand-up. You are not there to entertain a stranger. The fact that so many of these lines contain sexual innuendos means that women instinctively back off. Telling someone you just met how you'd like to wake up and have breakfast with them is alarming. Inviting a woman to sit on your face is not effective, it's offensive. If such a blatant sexual invitation leads to acceptance, recognize that you have likely stumbled upon a professional and that appropriate compensation will have to be paid.

The last thing you want to do is frighten someone or have them think that you are creepy. That shit gets around fast.

So here is the secret: there is no such thing as a pick up line. Just because you're laughed at a line in a magazine does not mean that it is the best thing to say to a woman whom you have just met.

The best opening line is simply, "Hi, my name is..."

That is sufficient. It is friendly. Non-threatening. No defenses will be thrown up because of its content. You will usually get a handshake if not the name of the person you have just greeted. A conversation has just started. In a little while, there will be an opportunity for humor. But now you are talking to someone, hopefully comfortably and there is no reason whatsoever to worry about how the pick-up line went over. Saying hello is innocent and the furthest from alarming that there is. No one will ever complain that the line is creepy. Starting the conversation at an acceptable social level where there can be friendly interaction may save you from doing things which appear to be creepy.

There is lots to talk about–you can start with the venue where you have found each other. Comments like "come here often?" are best left unsaid. "Is this place always this crowded/empty?" is a non-clichéd way of asking the same thing while avoiding the unspoken suggestion that she is an alcoholic if you're at a bar or that she goes out often to look for men.

So just go and introduce yourself and say hello.

It's that easy.

Having a wingman, that is, someone to watch your back, is often useful while sarging. It is not entirely necessary but sometimes you will find that a wingman is helpful. That's why talk show hosts have sidekicks. If a joke falls flat or things start to lag, the wingman's job is to get them going again.

Most helpful of all is a wingwoman. She can go up to a girl you'd like to talk to and say that she should talk to you. More often than not, the girl will do so. Even if she's married. Especially if she's married, for if she's happily married what is she doing out on the town? You may find yourself hearing women tell you that they just want to talk to their girlfriends. Undoubtedly, there are times when this happens. But when they are trying to get these same girlfriends to go out the enticement is that they will all meet new men.

If they really wanted to talk to each other they could go to a coffee shop where they probably wouldn't be bothered and could have all the private conversation they wanted. Or they could go to a restaurant with leafy palm fronds and spectacular salads. But they have not. They're sitting at the bar in a local saloon waiting to be approached.

The other extremely useful role a female

wingman plays is providing validation. You are hardly a sinister creep if accompanied by a friendly girl. This is the sisterhood's way of saying 'green light: you may approach.' Otherwise, having guy as a wingman is helpful for those situations when you are approaching more than one woman but you have a particular interest only in one. In these circumstances, remember not to be blinded by your lust–the one you are not all that attracted to may instead be attracted to you. Remember the puppy principle. Let it happen.

Another useful role for the female wingman is when you have been friend-zoned, or at least you believe you have been friend-zoned. If a woman has done this to you then there really is no reason that she should be jealous when you are out looking for sexual partners. So bring her along. If she finds that she is jealous then maybe that will be enough to get you out of the friend zone. And being in the friend zone with her may not be so bad when you have just met another woman. One-itis is a terrible condition and there is only one way to cure it. Why not let the author of that condition–your 'friend'–help you find a cure?

The main purpose of sarging is interacting with people. Each interaction will be different. Some will be outright flirting. Some may be a polite decline. But you never know what will happen. You just never know.

You don't need a wingman to sarge. You certainly can do it by yourself. But until you get the feel for it, it may be useful to have help.

One day my friend Cool Clyde called me up and asked me to meet him at Houston's. Clyde had just closed an important deal and I wanted to hear all about it.

Unfortunately, I knew that we would never discuss the deal but we would be sarging, since that is all Cool Clyde and I ever did together. I met Cool Clyde at an adult education class at the Alliance Francaise. This is an institution that provides continuing education classes for adults and children in French language and culture. But it is much more than just the classroom. There are wine tastings and social programs and all sorts of women–and men–who are tired of the bar scene.

As cool as he was, Cool Clyde always had difficulty making the first move. When I met him at Houston's he was eyeing two girls sitting at the bar, one black, the other Latin. I went up the Latin girl and asked her if she spoke Spanish. She was from Acre and spoke Portuguese, but she told me that her grandparents were from Paraguay. I happened to have a friend who knows a little Guaraní, Paraguay's second language. I excused myself, called him, and asked him for something to say to this beautiful creature. He said, "tell her this" and gave me a phrase. I went up to her and repeated the phrase. She looked at me and said, "that's how old people talk," but with a smile.

Next thing you know we're in the back seat of her car on the way to a black strip and rap club. She told me that she worked at Hooters. Cool Clyde was getting to know his new friend in the front seat.

When we arrived the place was packed. There was a huge line outside but a fifty-dollar bill got us in ahead of everyone else. Having two pretty girls with us didn't hurt, either. Unusually for a strip club, there were a lot of female customers in the audience. I guess they figured that since it was hard to date a dancer, the already horny guys might take interest in them. If there were just one of two, this strategy wouldn't work, but in this black club there were dozens. It's an interesting idea, ladies. Don't knock it till you've tried it. But Cool Clyde and I were the only two white guys there. The two girls knew several of the dancers and wanted us to buy dances from their friends. Why not? The point of this is that a simple hello during a sarge can lead to just about anything.

You don't have to restrict your sarging to nightclubs and bars. You can sarge at political events, wine tastings, gallery openings or other events.

Sarging can and will take you out of your

comfort zone. That is the point: your comfort zone is boring. From time to time you have to take risks. When opportunities come your way, get up and grab them.

CHAPTER 21

How to talk to Women

This is not rocket science. You tend to freeze up because you wonder if she can read your dirty, filthy mind. To an extent she can. Sorry. If your mind is creepy you will come off as creepy as well. It will affect the way you carry yourself, your mannerisms. It will make you hesitate when you should be bold. What will come through is your insecurity and insecurity is the last thing you want to show when making a new friend.

I came across a web post the other day which contained advice about how to talk to women. Here it is, unvarnished:

"[S]top thinking of them as women altogether. Imagine they're you're best guy friend and just clown around with them as you normally would."

From http://seanmeverett.quora.com/How-To-Talk-To-Chicks-For-Nerds.

In other words, ignore (if you can) the fact she is a woman. Treat her like a human being, like the friend she might become. Talk about those things that interest you as if you were talking with a guy. Talk about those things which you think might interest her as if you were talking to another guy. This will take the edge off and make it much easier.

Women know that men are simple creatures and the idea of sex is never far from our thoughts. Don't be worried about who and what you are. If she didn't want interaction she wouldn't be out and she wouldn't be talking to you. Keep in mind that word "interaction." Interaction does not mean sex, it just means talking to someone. If she doesn't want to talk to you she will let you know.

Otherwise, try to have a nice simple conversation about some passing subject of national or social interest. Celebrity news or opinion is always a winner and these days is cross-cultural. This is effective even if you are at a political gathering. You may be tempted–or your new friend may be–to talk about the Second Amendment or the latest political outrage. Keep it light and mention some tidbit of celebrity gossip instead. Is the new senator from Massachusetts really Native American? (Or First Nations, as they say in Canada?) Johnny Depp claims that he is. And what about that new movie, yada yada.

But don't forget to ask for her phone number.

CHAPTER 22

Phone Game

If a woman gives you her telephone number it doesn't mean that she wants to fuck you. All it means, and nothing more, is that she is open to further contact. You may find, however, that sometimes the number she gave doesn't exist, doesn't belong to her or has been disconnected. While there is a slight chance she misremembered her number or wrote it down incorrectly–this happens all the time with emails, by the way–more likely you have just found yourself on the receiving end of a graceful exit. When this happens, pick yourself up, dust yourself off and try with someone else.

If you do connect on the phone, what do you say? The magnificent game that you displayed a few days ago in person is a fading memory. Pretty girls get hit on all the time. She may remember you, but you may need to jog her memory as well. If you can recall something she said or something that the two of you talked about, so much the better. The problem is approaching this kind of a call as a business call. You are familiar with those, you make them every day. Business calls are not abstract—you have a purpose, maybe even a script and there is always something concrete you want to accomplish. If a call doesn't have a purpose, you don't make it. What is the content for a follow-up call to a girl you met just a few days before?

Phone game is key if there is ever going to be a second meeting. Since I was fourteen years old I have had difficulty talking to women on the phone. I'm too businesslike, too gruff. If a call doesn't have a purpose, you don't make it. It's very difficult to make a call when the true purpose of the call–I want to sleep with you–must be concealed/can't be revealed.

But what to say? Talking about the weather is what people do when they want to communicate but don't have anything to say. Talking about politics can quickly take you into unchartered waters and may yield unpleasant findings, no matter what side of the political seas you may find yourself on.

When I was a teenager I would pick up the phone to call a girl but hang up before she answered because my words just seemed to gag me. After "hi how are you?" there's not much to say. You can't just say, "Let's get together?"

You spend more time ordering a pizza. You simply can't say hello like you would in a bar or another social gathering where different cues or the environment provide either content or a starting point for conversation.

Phone game is difficult to study because usually you only have one side of the conversation. It's more difficult to anticipate what might be said and what might be useful come-backs. In short, my phone game sucked.

Then I met Rodrigo. Rodrigo is a master of phone game. I didn't know it when I met him and we were friends for years before I figured this out. How often do you get a chance to listen to your friends talk to women they want to date? If ever there was a need for a private phone booth, this is it.

But one afternoon during a football game Rodrigo picked up the phone and made five telephone calls. One after the other. To five different girls. Each call lasted about three minutes. So I listened to fifteen or twenty minutes of calls as the Dolphins did—well, as the Dolphins basically did nothing. As usual.

After he made the calls, I realized that I could not remember what he said. All I could say was that he was smiling and happy when he made the calls, that there was laughing and some joking, and before I knew it, the call had ended. Then I realized the secret: the calls had no content. They were just about sharing a good feeling or bringing back a good feeling that was there when they last met or before.

Every now and then there was a reference to the news or something going on–but not real news, light celebrity news or quirky events like the abandoned monkey at the Ikea store in Canada. So this is the key insight: you don't need content for a phone call. The purpose is just to share a pleasant feeling and then hang up before the feeling goes away. She will associate talking to you with pleasantness. No one wants to talk to a deb. So don't worry if you don't have content for your phone call or if you don't know what to say. Keep in mind:

- the conversation should be short

- no more than three minutes

- talk about getting together without making any definite plans

- keep some quirky fact in your back pocket if you need it.

So hey, how are you? What have you been up to? Are you going to take that cute outfit you had on the other night for a spin again? Let me know if you do. I'm sitting here watching the Dolphins, I really don't know why, they only know how to lose. Wish I had some wings. You want to get together for wings? I just said that, I don't like them. Haha. OK, I'll call you this week.

Rinse and repeat. Leave her with a good feeling. It doesn't matter that neither of you will remember what you talked about because if you did this right you didn't talk about anything.

Don't be afraid to pick up the phone.

CHAPTER 23

The Puppy Principle

I used to have an Akita that I raised after purchasing him from a breeder. I thought that the way you buy a dog is to go to a breeder and pick out one that you like. I was completely wrong. When I went to the kennel, I was ready to pick out a puppy that I liked. The breeder advised against this. The best way, she told me, is to sit with the puppies. If one jumps up on your lap and stays, that's your puppy. Let them select you. The Akita I came home with that day turned out to be a great dog.

Years later, I realized that this advice, which I call the "puppy principle" is one of the most important rules of dating.

147

In a target-rich environment, whether it be a bar, a party or an event, you can pick the puppy you want and trail her for a while only to realize after wasting time that she is not your puppy. The best approach is to wait for the puppy to come to you.

This does not mean that a woman is going to jump on your lap–though if this happens, congratulations. More likely, you will get an eye signal or some other expression of interest. Once this subtle invitation is received you can act on it.

This is a hundred times better than merely chasing after a woman you are attracted to. It's hard, granted, not to do so, especially after you have internalized some of the rules of this book and have no fear of rejection because you know that you cannot be rejected. You can be told "no", of course, but that's different. So wait. Sit still in the chair. Let the puppies see you, become comfortable with you. Let them sniff you. Let them determine that you are not a threat. And eventually look for a sign that one likes you. Now half the battle is over.

Why waste your time chasing women who have no interest in you? Things are so much better when you let the puppy principle operate and run its course.

Let them come to you. It may be difficult at first to pick up on the subtle signals, but they are there. Women do not go out to places where there are eligible men because they want to be alone. If a woman tells you that all she wants to do is talk to her girls it is because she is not attracted to you and is being polite. Otherwise, she might say, "stay and talk to us." After all, there is no reason why two puppies might not jump into your lap at the same time.

Remember that the puppy principle is one of the more important rules to keep in mind in any dating situation.

I was in the bar, the one down the street from my house. It was a Sunday night. When I walked in, the place was pretty much empty, except for a young woman who was sitting by herself at the corner of the bar.

I sat down at the bar. There was a bowl on the bar where customers had dropped business cards. I guess it was a promotion the bar ran, leave your card and earn a chance to win a free lunch. I picked up a handful from the bowl the cards swam in.

–Are any of these yours? She nodded no.

I introduced myself and we struck up a conversation. She had come because her girlfriend told her that the Argentine pop star Charly García sometimes went to the bar. I had never heard of Charly.

The conversation moved from Charly's music to movies and then was starting to lag. I could ask for her phone number and either she would give it to me or I would get shot down right there.

So, I said,

"Hey, tell me a secret."

She looked at me for a second and said, "My last relationship was with a woman."

I asked her why the relationship ended and

we kept talking and then there was another drink and then another. It wasn't long before we were holding hands walking back to my house.

When I took off her clothes in the living room she told me, "I'm not accustomed to this" and I thought that she meant one-night stands.

But she didn't.

The next day, I was trying to piece together what had happened, for obviously I had done something right. Looking back over the evening, what made everything change was that moment when I asked her to tell me a secret. I'd like to take credit for this, but I have to admit that it is possible that the hint came from somewhere else, now forgotten.

The key insight is this: when you meet someone new, you are a stranger. When they tell you a secret you are no longer a stranger. You are someone who knows their secrets.

This is the most powerful technique I have come across and it works in all walks of life. In discussing this with my friends, those students who come to me for dating help, I explain this insight and its power.

More than one woman I know has told me, "That's ridiculous. Why would I tell you a secret if I don't know you?" But they do. Perhaps a stranger is a perfect sounding board for a confession, like the anonymous priest in the confessional. The stranger doesn't know any of your friends, so he is safe to tell the secret to. But once you tell a stranger a secret, he is no longer a stranger.

The way to use the technique is this: just drop the phrase in casual conversation. As if it were just more banter, a phrase that could almost be ignored. There are two likely responses. The first is something along the lines of, "I'm not going to tell you a secret, I hardly know you." If that's her response, follow up with a reply like, "Wow, you must be hiding a lot," or "you must have a lot of secrets." Let it drop and don't bring it up until much later, when you can ask, "do you know me well enough now to tell me a secret?" You still might not get anything. Many women simply will not tell you a secret, or they will tell you something silly–"I'm Justin Bieber's secret girlfriend" that you can discount immediately. In those cases, just let it drop. No harm, no foul.

But in many other cases, your new friend will respond by telling you a secret. Ask her about it. Discuss it with her. It may be obvious by the nature of the secret why it is a secret but it may not. She may tell you why she needs to keep this secret. She may tell you of the whole episode that had to be kept secret. And when she's finished, you are no longer a stranger. You are someone on the inside of what was called the Circle of Trust in the Meet the Fokker movies. It's a cheesy cliché, but it's true.

There is a variation on the technique where you tell her, "well, if you won't tell me a secret, I'll tell you one." And then lie. This must be a good lie but it should be at least a little self-revealing. This is not the time to boast, but it's OK to exaggerate.

Good lies are always well seeded with the truth and facts that can be corroborated. Tell her how you used to be fat. Or good looking. Or whatever. The effect is somewhat forced, because now you've dragged her into your own circle of trust. At least this is how it will appear. In any event, a dynamic is set up that is no longer the dynamic of two strangers sitting at a bar, it's a dynamic of two people who have shared a secret.

I can't emphasize how useful and important this technique is.

CHAPTER 24

Kino

Ovid recognized the importance of kino in the first century AD:

> Fingers that say things can't be in-
> tercepted
> A nod too, can be noted and ac-
> cepted.
> Don't worry if the rows create a
> squash
> House rules compel you and the girl
> to touch.

Ovid, *Art of Love*, trans. By Thomas Payne (Vintage 2011)

What is kino? Kino is a word that the seduction community uses for strategic touching. This does not mean that you start touching strange women when you start talking to them. The law enforcement community has a word for such touching. The word is 'assault.' But there is nothing wrong with a friendly tap on the shoulder to get one's attention or slowly shaking hands when meeting or a hug when saying goodbye.

One of my favorite games to play is the staring game. After one or two successful games–if games and tests are what you're running–you ask your new friend to play yet another game, the staring game. In this game you have to stand close to each other while holding hands and stare in each other's eyes for fifteen seconds without laughing.

Fifteen seconds of dead time is an eternity and more than enough time for the game. Secondly, pretending is reality. When you pretend to be lovers, oxytocin is released. She will have a good feeling about you and she will have no idea where it comes from. If one of you laughs before the fifteen seconds are up, try again. Laughing is good and makes the serious nature of this game more playful.

Now that you have a pick-up line–whom do you talk to? There are a couple of options. Depending on the environment, you can simply do nothing and trust the puppy principle. When a woman approaches you, say hello and introduce yourself. This is a useful technique but it owes more to the power of the puppy principle than anything else.

The other option is to use the five second rule. This rule says that a woman who looks at you for more than five seconds may be interested. Five seconds can be a long time. If she smiles, so much the better.

One night I was at Houston's again with Cool Clyde. He was eyeing a group of ladies sitting across the U-shaped bar from us. He said that he wished he could talk to them. From time to time they would look at us, utterly ignoring the five second rule (its counterpart is that if you stare you're a stalker). I waved at one of the women who were looking at us and she waved back. So I got up off my barstool, walked over to her, introduced myself and made a new friend. Cool Clyde was amazed. He had been trying all evening to muster up the courage to walk over while trying to think of something clever to say.

That's the beauty of simplicity. You don't have to agonize over pithy comments that in any event will soon be forgotten, and if a woman is checking you out she'd like you to come over and say hello.

After we left the bar Cool Clyde asked me, "how did you do that?" He was truly astounded. But all I did was combine a rule with a friendly hello. Nothing more. Sometimes it's just that easy.

CHAPTER **25**

She's not the One

After you have had some success in turning your social life around, don't fall for the first woman you meet. You may think that all your problems are resolved. Meeting a really cool woman right after you've started going out again is one of the worst things that can happen to you. Why? Because you're not in a position to judge. You've been alone too long, or you're afraid that there will be a dry spell again when this relationship is over. You don't realize it, but mentally you are a trapeze artist and you don't want to let go of the swing.

You have met a woman who is accomplished and who is independent. One who pays attention to you. She is nice. You go out with her once or twice. The sex you start to have with her is good. Because you haven't been getting much lately, it's not just good sex, it's great sex.

You start thinking about her, wondering when you'll be able to be with her next. You stop sarging. Why should you keep putting yourself out there? You have a girlfriend now, right? Except that maybe she doesn't treat you in exactly the same way. You're a friend yes, a friend with benefits, you get together and have a great time. But she is cautious, she's been burned before, she will only go far. When she stays at your place she has no problem leaving late at night. Or if she does stay, she does the walk of shame wearing that tight black cocktail address right out the door at 8 am, despite your pleas for her to stay.But perhaps you think about her more than she thinks about you. Maybe you find yourself mooning after her like a teenager. The green-eyed monster invades your thoughts at inconvenient times.

You have a job, obligations, you can't be spending time wondering what this girl is thinking, who she is talking to, whether she is into you as much as you are into her.

You've got one-itis.

One-itis is a disease. It is one of the worst diseases you can get while trying to meet new women. A bout of one-itis can take you out of the game, return you to your den and your television swearing never to go out again. The disease is insidious, its approach subtle. Before you realize it, you are afflicted.

It may well be that this woman is for you. She may be the girl you meet in later life who is perfect in so many ways. Think of Paul McCartney's third wife compared to the financial catastrophe that was his second. This new girl you have met may be the one for you. Or she may not. Who are you comparing her to? A relationship you had in the past? The past is dead, it is gone.

When a buddy is suffering from one-itis, his friends have to give him the cure, and there is only one cure–go out sarging. Meet new women. Have a plan B. Have an alternate. Have more than one name in your Rolodex you can call.

So if the one-itis girl says she can't see you, fine. And let her know it's fine. You're not dependent on her. This book is not about relationship advice, it's about meeting new people. An attack of one-itis will keep you out of the game, will keep you from meeting new women. It will keep you from meeting that wonderful second woman or a third or maybe even the one you eventually decide to settle down with.

One-itis always strikes just as you've gotten back into the game. You're so thrilled that a woman has taken interest in you, has given her body to you, that you're blinded to everything else. She may indeed be the woman with whom you will have a great, long-term fulfilling relationship. Or she may not be. You have to put yourself into the position of being able to decide. That's why you decided to learn game in the first place.

Don't fall prey to this disease.

The only solution, and there really is only one solution, is: meet more women. When you are with someone else thoughts of your crush will diminish. This doesn't exactly do wonders for your relationship with the first woman, but a rebound relationship may not be the best thing for either of you. Other girls will get you through the desert until the next oasis. Staying in the game is a good way to keep your skills intact. After spending time and effort on your new self, you do not want to slide back into the self you used to be.

There is no reason to overdo it. If you haven't pledged exclusivity, does it exist? If the two of you haven't talked about it, it doesn't exist. You may think that it was an unspoken understanding but unless she has formally announced that she is not dating anyone else and that she feels you are special, don't believe it. Such a declaration may not mean anything anyway. Such is the give and take in love wars.

Sarging is the medicine. And when you meet the second woman, the first will know. Even if you don't tell her, she will know. She'll know because you're not contacting her or texting her 24/7, because you've given her the "going out with friends" excuse or you didn't call her at all. So maybe she will start to think that she could lose someone she values and so she needs to pay greater attention.

Jealousy is a feeling you have to get over. The last thing you want to do, especially if you are at the initial stages of a relationship is to pledge fidelity to someone you barely know. She probably feels the same way. You've just met and whether there is a spark or not does not necessarily mean that she is going to give up her own social life.

Unless you're going to make yourself exclusively available to her, it's unfair to expect a behavior from her that you're not willing to give yourself. That does not mean that the feeling isn't real or that it doesn't hurt. But you have to put it out of your mind. Preferably by getting together with another woman.

Jealousy can be a killer, especially if you thought that there was a chance for the two of you to have something serious. You see her with another guy or group of guys and your heart just drops in your chest. It is not easy to ignore these feelings but this is what you have to do. Reproaching her with accusations about her behavior is useless. Here's what she will say:

- You didn't see anything.

- You are the only one.

- I care about you.

- How could you think I care about those guys? They're gay.

- You're too jealous.

You will then feel bad even though there is a halfway decent chance you've just listened to a stream of just-invented lies. Lying is just another form of communication, but this is time to pay no attention. Let her prove it to you physically. If you are going to trust, as Reagan said, verify.

In the first two or three months of a relationship, accept these protests for the lies that they are. In the unlikely event they turn out to be true, good for you. It is always better to juggle two women than be lovestruck by one who will disappear leaving you alone.

CHAPTER 26

Sex on the First Date

Should you have sex on the first date? It's a complicated question. The general rule is wait until the third date. By then you've had a chance to make a more reasoned decision as to whether you really want to. Nelson Algren wrote, "Never sleep with a woman whose troubles are worse than your own." He almost stole Simone de Beauvoir from the great French philosopher, Jean-Paul Sartre. She too wanted an alpha male. Algren fit the bill.

Women generally believe that if they sleep with you on the first date that you will think they are sluts and think badly of them. While that is the stated objection, the real fear is that you will never call her again. As Courtney Love sang,

"When they get what they want, they never want it again."

This is the real issue, no matter what anyone says it is.

An article in a recent English newspaper–written by a woman–condemned this line of thought and advocated freedom between the parties to shag upon first meeting. Perhaps it is nostalgia for the Free Love 60's, but those days are over for people over 50, right?

Maybe not. The college hook-up scene is as close to the Free Love 60's (and the hangover 70's) as you can get. Unfortunately, there are few sexually frustrated college girls who are going have men in their 50's on their speed dial. But "not many" means that a few will.

So while our cultural standards suggest that sex on the first date or the one night stand are bad ideas, we also know that such sex can be incredibly hot. When you start down that path it is very, very difficult to pull back and stop yourself and it is more difficult than you think for her to put the brake on things and say no.

On one splendid occasion, I was standing at the bar feeding finger foods from a small-plate entrée to a woman I had just met with a Basque-sounding name at Tu Tu Tango, now a defunct restaurant at Cocowalk. There is something about the moment–you just know. The Goddess of Lust descends and next thing you know you're taking her by the hand to the Men's Room, throwing a ten dollar bill at the attendant to buy his silence, and then bending her over the throne while shutting the stall door behind you.

And then you're walking out together from the men's room, hand in hand, as if nothing had happened. Sometimes the Goddess demands that rules be broken and you fail to do so at your peril.

The next afternoon, still severely hung over, I called her because while I can be accused of many things I am a gentleman. I referred to the great night that we had had, and told her I had just gotten up. "I've been up for hours," she said, "I had to get up early to feed the baby."

Baby? What baby? Somehow the subject didn't come up the night before. With a one night stand you never really know what you're getting. You might have to get up early to feed the baby.

An often repeated rule is "don't sleep together till the third date." You won't find this rule written down in any authoritative law book, but that makes it no less binding. When free sex was the norm in the 1960's, nobody even bothered to ask the question. By the time the 70's hangover hit, both men and realized that perhaps, maybe, sleeping with someone immediately after you've met them is a bad idea.

While both men and women complain about the rule, breaking it has consequences. It is interesting that both women and men are heard to complain about the constraints of the rule. A recent article in London's *Tele-*

graph provocatively questioned, "Why can't women be sluts?" Perhaps this is the new liberation. Certainly the younger generation with its hook-up culture, pays no mind to this rule. Or do they? What appears to be promiscuous, carefree sex at schools and universities has for the most part always been the norm. Whether things were on the down low or not depended on the mores of the time. People really don't change.

Justification for the rule can be found in another bit of advice: Don't sleep with someone who has more problems than you. But if you've just met them, how would you know?

Like it or not, the rule is there. You can't ignore it. And simply because you have decided that the rule doesn't apply to you doesn't mean that your new friend is not intensely aware of it, and despite her desire, does not want to be considered a slut by someone she has just met—you. Someone she likes. Pressuring her at this point isn't a good idea and may have consequences later on. Courtship has its many rituals and this is one of them.

There's an important ancillary rule which applies to some of us, which is not to reveal any kinks before the fifth date. After all, you don't want to frighten someone–or be scared yourself–by something that appears to be a bit outré. That is, unless it is obvious that both of you are in the same scene, whatever that scene may be. It is a big world out there, and whatever you imagine to be your strange fetish probably has a web site, mailing list, fan club and an affinity credit card. Whatever you imagine to be abnormal probably isn't.

Statistically infrequent, perhaps. But if you have made it to this stage in life without an arrest you already know how to tread cautiously in these areas. If a woman says, "you wouldn't know what to do with a girl like me," you probably don't. But if she tells you, "people like us always find each other" while discussing plate jobs, the kink rule probably can be safely ignored.

CHAPTER 27

Take it Off-Line

The number of relationships which commence on-line is increasing by the day. While the virtual world is fine for making initial connections, it is also a dangerous tar pit which has the tendency to trap the unwary. Never lose sight of the fact that the Internet should be for making initial contact only. Long texts, constant texts, e-mails, tweets, Viber or Skype SMS's, the constant back and forth all lead to nothing. These are useful tools to set up a date but that's it. Don't try to get to know the person on line. Do that in person. On line there is too much of a risk of being misunderstood.

Back in the day you could write letters back

and forth to a loved one and try to keep a relationship alive. Back then, letters meant something. Receiving one was an event. Now they are an anachronism. Letters are for business or communicating with the government. You do not have a relationship with someone you just became acquainted with on the Internet. So sending letters, or their contemporary electronic equivalents, simply do not work. In fact, they work against you. Use technology to arrange meetings or communicate about a meeting that has just taken place (as in saying thank you) or point out that you're looking forward to seeing someone again is completely acceptable.

When this graduates to five or more electronic pokes a day, you are embarking on a trip you don't want to take.

When you fall in love you can't get enough of the other person. They call it new relationship energy. You want to be with them all day, you think of them all the time. You express this longing through communication and start sending tweets or texts or e-mails or whatever on multiple occasions throughout the day. You get upset if your text isn't responded to immediately. Because you usually can't gauge emotions in such short messages, miscommunication becomes almost a certainty.

Because you don't have a relationship with someone you just met on the Internet, communication should be at a minimum. Once I made this mistake.

The woman was the sensitive, sentimental, literary type. She was an otherwise intelligent, conservative physician. A responsible citizen. She started sending long emails. If it wasn't a long e-mail, it was an SMS. Or a chat. But it was always something. It got to the point where I had to ask, "don't you have a job?" It seemed that she did nothing more to do each day than communicate with me. Then came my biggest error. When she wrote and asked, "do you think you could write me an erotic letter?" I thought, sure, why not? It was a huge mistake.

When I realized that I was unlikely to ever make it to the small town where this woman lived–Gonzalez, Texas–I told her that it was best that we don't communicate any more. She took this badly, even though I have–and still– never met this woman in person. I never slept with her. I did not betray her or play her.

Nevertheless, I ended up with a stalker. The stalker started calling up family members asking if I had been in an accident–I must have been, because I hadn't responded to her e-mails. The stalker called my aged aunt in a nursing home with the false report of my demise.

Of course, this caused a good deal of trouble for me. All of this led to this lesson: use the Internet wisely. For dating, get off the Internet and arrange a meeting as soon as possible.

And never, ever write love letters to lonely women.

CHAPTER **28**

Compensated Dating

Courtesans

In many societies there is a stigma that attaches to men who visit prostitutes. Some societies are more tolerant than others. The women you want to date will take a dim view of such behavior. In most cases, it is a horrible deal-breaker: if a woman finds out that you have gone to a prostitute even once you are forever cursed: there is no forgiveness.

The word "prostitute" or the term "prostitution" still has a sting. In Japan, the practice is simply known as compensated dating. Women who are compensated for dating also suffer a terrible stigma if they are caught. Discretion is the name of the game.

When business is slow at the workplace, you hire a consultant. The same applies here. If business is slow, consider hiring an "intimacy consultant."

The oldest profession has, nevertheless, permuted into new forms thanks to the Internet. It is no longer necessary to find women on the street protected by pimps. There is no need to have contact with the criminal element. Police stings and community clean-ups are common. In Miami even a judge was captured in such a sting, after offering $20 for a blowjob in the front seat of his SUV to an undercover policewoman.

While Craigslist has removed its 'adult services' section, working girls still advertise in the 'Casual Encounters' section. Chicago Magazine recommended placing an ad in the "Men Seeking Women" section and using the word 'generous,' such as "Generous Businessman in town for one night, seeking company. Send picture."

Backpages.com has somehow avoided the national attention paid to Craigslist and still runs escort and massage ads. Whether there will be a crackdown is anyone's guess.

Then there are the grey areas. Seekingarrangement.com is a site for women who wish to have an ongoing financial relationship with a man and list their monthly dollar amount requirements. While some of the advertisers delude themselves into thinking that the site is a charity, most of the women who advertise consider themselves good girls and are just dipping their toes into the pool of compensated dating. Another example of this phenomenon is sugardaddyforme.com. There are many other similar sites. These sites contain profiles of women who will be happy to date you for cash. It's somehow refreshing to see a woman honestly admit that she is selling her company, for say, one thousand dollars per month. The business end of the transaction seems so much cleaner when compared to the meretriciousness of the divorce courts.

Cool Clyde loves to seek arrangements. While most of the women who advertise there want an ongoing relationship of some kind–while saying that they have boyfriends, they want nothing sexual, etc.–Clyde has dated several women on the site for ultra-short periods of time–say a weekend, or even one night. I think this is because the rules expected of both parties for a relationship in which a woman is kept are too fluid. Neither men nor women really know what is expected of the other in such an arrangement. Obviously there will be disappointments. Men are simply going to pay cash out of the kindness of their hearts for nothing. If a kept woman has a boyfriend she is going to keep his existence away from her older, part-time boyfriend.

After women dip their toes into the compensated dating pool they may decide to go for a swim. There are all kinds of escorts, independent, those who work for an agency, full-time, part-time, university students, schoolteachers, girls on vacation and others with full-time jobs who want a little more excitement and even those who write books or blogs or make films about their exploits, such as the scientist in the U.K. behind the Belle de Jour blog, books and television series.

Cool Clyde told me about the criminal justice student he met while on a business trip. He ran an ad on Craigslist and within an hour had a few responses. She hoped to get her degree and become a police officer. I guess she wanted to practice going undercover.

Many of these women will offer what their ads call the "girlfriend experience" or "GFE." In this scenario your paid date will pretend to be your affectionate girlfriend for a few hours. Fights over money, poker nights with your friends and forgetting your anniversary are not part of the package.

There is something else called the "PSE" or "pornstar experience" but this for the most part is hyperbole. If she drops to her knees to blow you immediately after you've opened your door or just after you said hello, then you're getting the PSE.

Clyde claims that he only calls escorts when he is on business trips and really doesn't have the time–or the energy–to run game. He also claims that he just visits working girls when he's suffering from a dry spell and can't get a date. Clyde has also successfully turned a few of his short-time relationships into long-time girlfriends.

The older guy is the target market for compensated dating. Many escorts will not entertain younger customers. Whether you like it or not, this industry is aimed at you.

There are dangers to compensated dating, at least in the United States. First, there is the risk of arrest and subsequent exposure. While many working girls know that most of their customers are married, there is no surer way to end a marriage then to get caught in a prostitution sting.

Apart from the criminal justice implications, starting to visit prostitutes regularly will make it difficult to have other relationships with women and will definitely hurt your game. This is a major risk for older men. With age we become impatient. After you've gotten shot down a few times–and you will–you start to think, "the hell with this, I can go on eros.com and have a woman gratefully playing with me in a few hours." Soon you may think, "why should I run game at all?" Or worse, "why should I have a relationship at all?"

Despite what the haters say, game is not an end in itself. Going out and meeting women and getting their phone numbers and then not calling them because it was so much fun getting their numbers is stupid.

The point of game is meeting new people. The point of game, and let it be said, is a relationship with a woman. The techniques shown here and taught by others are useful when it comes to getting over shyness and meeting women. Whether we want to admit it or not, all of these tactics are designed to lead to a relationship.

If you want to avoid the risk of arrest in

your own country, the easiest way is to get on an airplane and travel to a place where the laws are more lenient. While there is no shortage of compensated daters in Las Vegas, in Clark County prostitution is illegal. Not so in Canada, Mexico, or many other countries in the hemisphere. Sexual tourism is big business. In other countries this behavior is not as stigmatized as it is in the United States. Thailand has made this into a big business. Soi Cowboy, a street in Bangkok full of strip clubs and hooker bars, has been in operation for sixty years. Women who come to the big city from the rural provinces are looked upon with great respect when they return after a few years in the city with enough money to purchase a home, a farm, and marry. The modern-day versions of the ancient courtesans are alive and well in Japan and China. While the U.S. Navy bases have long since shut down in the Philippines, the bars and clubs which sprung up to service the sailors are, for the most part, still in business.

The trafficking of women in third-world countries is a real problem. You should not contribute to the exploitation of women. If you want to have sex with children you will go to jail. This behavior is against the law in almost every country and is a violation of U.S. law. Otherwise tolerant countries will quickly become authoritarian hell-holes if you break these rules. So don't even think about it.

Tourism

Many people who go to Venice wonder at its sights but complain that it is too full of tourists. They hope to find the "real" Venice–it's there somewhere, but the fact of the matter is that Venice has been "full of tourists" for four hundred years. In the 1500's people were already complaining. The American writer Mary Morris famously pointed out that "the tourist Venice is Venice."

The reason why I point this out is that there is nothing wrong to embrace a place for what it is. For better or for worse, there are certain places on the globe that have pursued the sex tourism business, more so than others. Much travel advertising plays on our desires to visit a libidinous place where anything goes. "What happens in Vegas, stays in Vegas." Air Jamaica ads features a beautiful woman on the beach in Negril—what is being sold, Jamaica or the woman?

Sexual tourism is condemned in the West because of the exploitation of women. BBC documentaries expose Romanian snakeheads who sell women into sexual slavery on false promises of waitressing jobs in Spain or France. Governments are right to prohibit this trade. But there is another side to the story.

Can you classify the poor trafficked Romanian woman in the same category as a secretary who decides to seek adventure and make a little money on the side? One woman told me once, "if you're OK with casual sex, why not get paid for it"? In Japan, the term for this activity is not prostitution but "compensated dating."

In the United States, prostitution is almost universally illegal (even in Las Vegas). Canada allows the trade, but like the United Kingdom prohibits pimping and living off the proceeds of a prostitute. The Netherlands permits prostitution under a more or less strict regulatory regime.

Some countries have acquired a certain amount of notoriety because of this trade. There is much negative publicity. You make a mistake if you judge an entire country by what is really a minuscule part of its economy. The red light districts across the border in Mexico have been notorious for more than a hundred years. I do not mean to single out any country by including them in this chapter, but where these industries have been created to accommodate the older traveler, there is no reason not to take advantage of all the services offered.

There are many countries in the Western

hemisphere which sponsor such scenes. Mexico offers direct flight connections. But the stellar performer in northern Latin America is the scene around the Del Rey Hotel in the country's capital, San José, and the famous Blue Marlin bar. The Blue Marlin has been open since at least the 1980's and attracts not only local talent but girls from Panama, Colombia, Mexico and places further south.

Panama has been a popular port since the California Gold Rush and a local industry grew up to provide services to those transiting the Canal. During World War II, the U.S. was fearful of a Japanese invasion that would destroy the Canal. An entire division was sent to Panama to protect the waterway, but the invasion never came. The soldiers had nothing to do so they handed out shovels and told them to start excavating a new set of locks. One of the bars that was established to provide female company for the soldiers, the Blue Goose, is still in operation today.

Medellin, Colombia has the reputation of

hosting the most beautiful women in Colombia, if not in Latin America. Moving further south, you might learn of the secret of the treasures of Santa Cruz, Bolivia where the ladies are astonishingly beautiful. Santa Cruz is not a cold Andean city but sits in a lowland basin that is a center of agriculture and a crossroads for trade with Brazil. Before the cocaine trade exploded in the late 1970's, Santa Cruz was a place where wealthy Miami businessmen flew down on weekends for hunting. Today there is hunting of a different kind.

Buenos Aires, I am told, is worth a visit. Cuba is off-limits for Americans so Canadians and Europeans have to pick up the slack. Perhaps Tim Horton's will set up a branch in Havana if they don't have one already.

Despite the U.S. embargo, there are more flights to Cuba from Miami than to New York. These are reserved for Cuban Americans only. A recent visitor told me that while things have calmed down since the 'special period' in the early 90's when you could see *jiniteras* patrolling the streets looking for customers, that many delightful experiences can still be found. Whatever happened to "all men are created equal?" When it comes to flights to Cuba, some Americans are more equal than others. If you're not that kind of a hyphenated-American, island delights can be found in the Dominican Republic. There's lot's of fun to be had in Santo Domingo. If you want to get out of the capital, a bus line with gorgeous "bus attendants" plies the island from north to south. Many Americans are pleasantly surprised by the talent pool in the DR, and there are Jet Blue direct flights from New York.

Compensated dating is legal in the Netherlands and Germany. In Germany there are sex clubs—think upscale strip clubs with benefits–which advertise on the sides of buses. In England, it is illegal to live off the earnings of a prostitute but compensated dating itself is not prohibited. So escort services operate in a gray area. In Spain there are sex clubs with take out.

Arriving in Asia you have Thailand, where

an industry grew up long ago to accommodate the visitor. In some neighborhoods in
Bangkok it is impossible to walk down the
street without being solicited for a not so ther-
apeutic massage.

The Bangkok scene is hardly limited to side-
street massages. There are bars and bar girls
and a mall devoted to sex. There is a street
called Soi Cowboy, named after an African-
American bar owner who remained in South-
east Asia after the end of the Viet Nam war and
a formerly seedy street where scandalous sex
shows involving unusual objects were on offer.
While the shows linger on, the street is now
more well known for the nighttime flea market
there.

Until you make it to Bangkok you may find
the idea of paying a woman for sex to be re-
pulsive. If you feel this way, don't go. There
are many without this hang-up who feel that
Bangkok is paradise. Some feel that it is OK
to more overtly pay for sex when you are between girlfriends. Others are afraid that pay-

ing means they are admitting that they are no longer attractive to women. One way or another you pay. At my divorce arbitration I looked around the room. My lawyer, $300 per hour. The mediator, another $300. Her lawyer, $400. Everyone expected me to pick up the check. Maybe this is not paying for sex, but with the taxi meter ticking away at $1000 per, it's not a time for cool reflection.

Don't worry about paying. One way or another, you pay. There is one downside to compensated dating. You will get spoiled. Your skills will deteriorate. Your game will start to go. You will no longer need flirtatious banter nor good game, there is no need to have any game at all when you can rent the girlfriend experience for a few bills. As your skills atrophy meeting women will become more and more difficult.

The other danger is that you fall into a world where you don't belong. It's one thing to eat at a restaurant but working in the kitchen is a whole other story. Business girls are human beings. They can be sexy beautiful women whom you are attracted to. If you start seeing one on a regular basis, emotional attachments can develop. Certain worlds just do not mix.

If you're a Bukowski sitting on a bar stool surrounded by low-lifes it probably doesn't make much difference if that has always been your world. If all the women you have ever known have been on the game or part-timers or not adverse to taking money for sex, then your worlds have already mixed. But if you realize you can never take your new Fight Club friends to the office then you are straddling two different worlds. Don't try to mix them.

As I write this, Xiang Fei is sleeping in the next room. Her pimp, Mama Wu, has threatened her if she does not turn over the sum of $1000. Xiang Fei does not want to pay. She came to me and asked for help. She even offered to pay me. I turned down the offer of cash while trying to figure a way to help her get out of town. It would be awkward were Xiang Fei to appear at my multinational day job with a Triad gangster in tow. Still, Mama Wu does not want to mix worlds either and she knows that she can only thrive in the shadows. It would be best not to offer Xiang Fei asylum, but sometimes a player has to do what he's gotta do.

And it was worth it just to hear her offer to pay me. How many times does that happen in real life?

I have just mentioned a few places in the world where you might experience some real adventures and hopefully without the threat of a Mama Wu knocking at your door. You may find the places I've mentioned boring; you may prefer a family golfing holiday in Cancun. But you no longer have a family, my friend, those days are over. That's why you are reading this book. Those days may come again, but not right now. In the meantime, explore and enjoy. And may a Mama Wu never darken your door.

Mail Order Brides

Paul was married for twenty years. His wife died before their twenty-first anniversary. He was by himself for a while before he decided that he really, really needed to get married again. He didn't meet anyone; he was shy and awkward and not really willing to make the investment of time going out to places to meet women randomly.

There were a couple of options for Paul. There are services such as selectivesearch dot com. These services recruit women who are interested in marrying wealthy, but not necessarily older, men. Once I was sitting in a hotel in Ft. Lauderdale wondering why there was such a parade of beautiful women into the lobby, one after another, at intervals of about a half hour. Finally I went up to the woman who was meeting them, and she told me that she had traveled from Chicago for interviews. Men pay $5000-$6000 and more for such introductions. The women are commitment- and marriage-minded and so are the men.

There are also services that provide introduction to women from other countries. Russia and Colombia are two that come to mind, but these are far from being the only ones. Paul married a twenty-two year old Russian woman. They signed a pre-nuptial agreement that gave her increasing rights the longer she stayed in the marriage. After three years they would agree to divorce and he would buy her a condominium in her country.

It worked out to be a very satisfying three years for Paul. After that, he and his new bride split on amicable terms that had been agreed to beforehand. Paul told me that he was interested in extended the arrangement but she did not want to. He has just started to interview new candidates.

There are legal issues with prenuptial agreements of this type. They may not be valid in your state. Bringing a young wife home to the United States is not as easy as you would think. The Government wants you to prove that it is a "real" marriage. The only incontrovertible evidence they will accept is if you have a child with your new bride, and that's asking a lot. Not all countries are as paranoid as the United States is on this issue so depending on where you live, this may not be an issue. Most other countries merely want to see a valid marriage certificate, and the inquiry stops there.

Keep in mind that a fish out of water will not survive. Your wife may be vivacious and happy in her home country. Once she has been separated from her family and friends she may be utterly depressed and bored in yours. There's not much you can do if that starts to happen except to offer her a ticket home. There are many stories of these relationships going sour after the wife learns English, obtains her green card and decides she no longer needs the man who brought her over. That is why a time-limited pre-nupe is a good idea.

Chapter 29

Recreational Pharma

No book about dating and the older man would be complete without a discussion of recreational drugs. By these I do not mean cocaine, ecstasy, meth, the 70's favorite, quaaludes, or any other illegal drug. By this I mean the big three, Viagra, Levitra and Cialis.

Let's face it, physically we are not what we were thirty years ago. You can struggle along with the awkward highs and lows or you can turn to the wonders of modern science. It astounds me that guys who take blood pressure medication every day are "too macho" to admit that from time to time they pop the little blue pill. There is no shame in this.

When I was a younger consultant I was assigned a male secretary. Let's call him Don. Don wasn't like anyone else in the consultancy. He carried a gun to work every day in a leather portfolio. This was Miami, true, but still. Back then they had not passed the concealed carry law but Don didn't particularly care. He was in his 70's and had flown DC-3's over the Hump to Burma in World War II. Don had a 40-something girlfriend, what he called a "shackjob." Don had also had cancer and had his prostate removed.

"I got the pump," he said. "It's unbelievable. If anyone ever suggests to you that you should get it, don't hesitate. Don't wait a second. It's great. It's like I'm 16 again. A few squeezes and I'm good to go."

Don had Social Security and a government pension. He didn't need to work, and he certainly didn't need to work for a newbie like me. Don was not about to withdraw into the sedentary life of a senior citizen. Whatever adversity he faced, it was nothing compared to the life and death challenges of the Second World War. Don wanted to keep wrestling life.

This is a drastic remedy, but one that had at least one very satisfied customer. Years later, another guy in his 70's told me about the shot. I think he was in his 70's. He told me that was his best guess. The issue came up when a federal judge asked him how old he was and he answered by saying that he couldn't be completely sure. I thought he was just being a smart-ass, but then he went on and said that in rural Florida at the beginning of the century, black babies weren't always given birth certificates. This was another guy who may have been 70 but he lived 40 and looked a lot less than his years.

He told me that the shot was a small needle–think along the lines of a thumbtack–that you injected yourself with which immediately caused an erection. The use of the term "inject yourself" made me run for cover–all I could think of was the huge vaccination needles from childhood or heroin addicts shooting up. A pinprick is much closer to the reality.

These two measures provide guaranteed success. The surgery required for the pump is not for everyone, but the option is out there. The shot may be your last resort, but you are only going to be able to use it under a doctor's supervision. You can't purchase this stuff over the counter. For that matter, you can't buy Viagra over the counter either, at least not yet. Outside of the United States or Canada it's less of an issue.

For the rest of us, the big 3 are the drugs of choice. The first time you use them you probably will not feel that you really need them. But what they will do is take the worry about being able to perform away, and since at least half of male sexual performance is mental–and these three will not work unless you are aroused mentally, that's half the battle.

As to which of these drugs is the best, I cannot say. My advice is to experiment. Like any other drug, if you just use one eventually you will build up a tolerance. So why not pick and choose amongst all three?

Younger men use these drugs too. The main reason is because they've been drinking too much or taking other drugs which affect performance so they too need to take the little blue pill. As time goes on and the population ages the stigma which first attached to these drugs is slowly disappearing as people come too accept that they are nothing more than recreational drugs.

Dr. Bob is an physician who lives in Cambodia. He introduced me to Human Growth Hormone, (HGH) a performance-enhancing drug that is banned by baseball and by many other sporting associations. Dr. Bob said that he prescribes HGH mainly for his older patients. As we get older, the level of HGH in the body decreases. Our skin starts to thin. At age 50, you're not going to see much in the way of results. Dr. Bob says his patients start seeing good results around age 60, but the dramatic results are found in his patients over 70. HGH is available only by prescription, unless you happen to be in Cambodia. It has be be refrigerated and you have to inject it. This sounds worse than it is; you don't inject it into a vein and because the needle is small it feels no worse than a pinprick.

What does the future hold? Other drugs are in the works and as the patents expire there will be new and improved versions brought to market. Some studies have shown that cocaine can cause spontaneous erections in new users, but the effect goes away with time. This might explain why cocaine drags so many people in. Australian researchers have found that melanin can have the same effect when injected–and has the beneficial side effect of making you less susceptible to sunburns.

Currently, pharmaceutical companies are promoting the sale of testosterone injections and inviting men to come in to specialized clinics to see if they have "Low T." Some men swear by these injections while others worry about the side effects. On the other hand, if you read the package insert of any kind of medicine you wouldn't take it unless it were a life or death situation. Once you start taking taking these shots, you have to take them, well, until you don't have to take anything anymore. It's a lifetime commitment, which is why Big Pharma is so keen on the concept. At the moment, the jury is still out.

There will be many sexual enhancement drugs in the future. What is really needed is a similar-type libido enhancing drug for women. When Viagra was first introduced in the market, some women took it and praised its benefits. Later, it turned out that Viagra does not work in women in the same way it works in men. These women were experiencing the placebo effect. The placebo effect, though, is real. These women let us know that they should not be left out of the search for this class of effective recreational drugs. I can only hope that the pharmacologists vigorously pursue this research.

CHAPTER 30

The Future

Whether this is your purpose or not, all of these interactions lead to relationships of one kind or another. The relationship may be exclusive or it may not. You may want to jump out of the frying pan of divorce into the fire of another committed relationship. The rebound relationship may be fleeting. Or it may last a couple of months. It could well last longer, even years.

Whatever happens, it will be up to the two of you. I am not going to take a misogynistic view of things and say avoid long-term relationships so that you can stay in the game. The game is fun, but it is a means to an end and not an end in itself. You may decide that you want to be leave yourself open to one encounter after another. Or you may decide that you want something more. How you accomplish that is beyond the scope, as consultants are famous for saying.

I have no advice for you about maintaining or nurturing relationships. That is something for others with expertise far beyond my own.

Maybe I should do some research.

Good luck, my friend. A new world awaits you.

CHAPTER **31**

For Further Reading

Anon. *The Arabian Nights* (9th Cent) trans. Richard Burton, Modern Library 2004

Anon, *Chin P'ing Mei (The Golden Lotus)* (16th Cent.) translated as Don Juan of China, Rutland Press 1960.

Casanova, Giacomo, *Story of My Life*, (1798), trans. Willard Trask, Johns Hopkins University Press 1997

Choderlos de Laclos, Pierre *The Dangerous Liaisons*, (1782), tran. Helen Constantine, Penguin 2007

DeAngelo, David, *Double your Dating*, doubleyourdating.com

Gracián, Baltasar, *The Art of Worldly Wisdom* (1637), trans. Joseph Jacobs, Dover 2005

Greene, Robert , *The Art of Seduction*, Profile Books 2004

ibn Hazm, Ali (1064), *The Ring and the Dove: A Treatise on the Art and Practice of Arabian Love*, Trans. A.V. Arberry, (London) Luzac 1953

Jeffries, Ross, *Secrets of Speed Seduction*, 1994

de Molina, Tirso, (1630), *The Trickster of Seville* (*El burlador de Sevilla*) trans. Gwynne Edwards, Aris Phillips 1986

von Markovik, Erik, Mystery, /The Mystery Method, St. Martin's Press 2007

Ovid, *The Art of Love*, (First Cent.)   trans. Thomas Payne, Vintage 2011

Strauss, Neil,*The Game: Penetrating the Secret Society of Pick-up Artists*, Harper-Collins 2005

Weber, Eric, *How to Pick Up Girls!* Symphony Press 1970

Casanova's Threesome Tip

The only outright tip that Casanova writes about in his memoirs isn't about meeting women but how to get two women to participate in a threesome. Neil Strauss writes about this as well in *The Game.* When you are with two women and the three of you are trying to decide what happens next, Casanova suggests asking the two girls which of them is the biggest prude. He found that each would claim that the other was and Casanova would then ask one to prove it, and from there things would slowly escalate.